STATIONS OF THE CROSS

Stations of the Cross

Flor McCarthy
Miriam Pollard
Gerard Mackrell
Seán P. Kealy
June Johnston & Glenroy Taitt
Conor O'Riordan

DOMINICAN PUBLICATIONS

This edition first published (1991) by
Dominican Publications
42 Parnell Square
Dublin 1

Reprinted February 2001

ISBN 1-871552-12-5

British Library Cataloguing in Publications Data.
A catalogue record of this book is available
from the British Library.

Cover design by David Cooke

Origination by Dominican Publications

Printed by The Leinster Leader Ltd, Naas, Co. Kildare

Contents

Stations of the Cross

Flor McCarthy

Foreword

No one has to go looking for suffering. Sooner or later it knocks at everybody's door. I believe far too much emphasis has been placed on suffering as the will of God. This has given rise to an unquestioning resignation in the face of things and conditions which could and should be changed. 'What is called resignation is confirmed desperation' (Thoreau).

God does not want us to suffer, no more than parents want their children to suffer. Nor did he want his Son to suffer. The Passion was not something which Christ had to go through because his Father demanded it from him. It was something he freely chose. 'No one takes my life from me; I lay it down of my own free will' (Jn 10:18).

Christ suffered because he was faithful to the task his Father had given him – to be a shepherd to his flock. He was that Good Shepherd who, through love, lays down his life for his sheep.We are saved not by his suffering but by his love.

It follows that what Christ wants from us his followers is not our suffering but our love and faithful witness. The Christian vocation challenges us to be people who love, who care, and therefore who suffer as Christ suffered. However, sometimes the only witness we may be able to give is to suffer patiently.

Christ was no spectator, no critic, standing on the sidelines of life. He shared the human condition fully. He took on himself the burden of all human suffering. He is the guarantee that pain, suffering, loss, and death do not separate us from God, but bring us closer to him. They are not the end, not the last word.

He suffered for us and still suffers in us. But this does not mean that he takes away our pain. No one, not even Christ, can suffer in our place. What Christ does is make it possible for us to transform our suffering into a thing of value. He helps us to bear it in a way that purifies and spiritualizes us.

All sufferers can draw comfort, strength, and hope from the Passion of Christ. But I think that two categories of people can draw special inspiration from it.

The first category consists of the poor. 'When you are poor you feel at home in the Passion. The Passion is so close to the poor. Every station reflects a little piece of your life' (Catherine de Hueck Doherty).

The second category consists of those who suffer precisely because they are disciples of Christ. In some parts of the world Christians are still being called upon to make the supreme sacrifice. In other parts, however, they have to do something which may be even harder – to witness before an indifferent world.

The Passion still goes on, not in Christ, but in us. The following of Christ's path to Calvary will help us to bear our cross, whatever form it takes, with patience and dignity. May it also open our eyes to those who suffer around us and move us to do what we can to help them.

This is no pious Way of the Cross. I have tried to insert it into the modern world, a world in which a lot of ugly things happen. May we so celebrate it that our stories merge with that of Christ. Then, having suffered with him, we may hope to be glorified with him too.

Flor McCarthy

Suggestions for Use

There is far too much material here for a single celebration of the Way of the Cross. It is up to the leader or planner of the celebration to make a selection in advance.

For instance, it would be too much to use all the psalms at one time. One here and one there would be sufficient. In between the intercessory prayers can be used.

Incidentally, the intercessory prayers given in the text are only examples of the kind which could be said. Wherever possible the participants should be given an opportunity to make their own spontaneous prayers. This will help them to enter more personally into the story.

Sometimes instead of the meditation given for a particular station one of the reflections might be used. Pauses for silence are suggested at significant moments and should be availed of.

For the sake of variety two or more voices could be used in reading the meditations. Likewise, different participants could be asked to lead the psalms being used.

The whole idea is to enable as many people as possible to participate actively rather than being mere listeners. The extra material provided means that the book can be used several times with the same group.

Introduction

Let us start this Way of the Cross by listening to a reading from
Scripture.   *[Three options are given below.]*

Option One

A reading from the Gospel according to John   10:11-15
>   Jesus said:
>   'I am the good shepherd:
>   the good shepherd is the one who lays down his life for
>   his sheep.
>   The hired man, since he is not the shepherd
>   and the sheep do not belong to him,
>   abandons the sheep and runs away
>   as soon as he sees a wolf coming,
>   and then the wolf attacks and scatters the sheep;
>   this because he is only a hired man
>   and has no concern for the sheep.
>   I am the good shepherd;
>   I know my own and my own know me,
>   just as the Father knows me and I know the Father;
>   and I lay down my life for my sheep.'
>   This is the Gospel of the Lord.

[Pause]

The Passion was not something which Christ had to undergo. It
was something he freely chose. He suffered because he cared
about the flock his Father had entrusted to him. We are saved not
by his suffering but by his love.

What Christ wants from us is not our suffering but a life of love
and service. But of course such a life will inevitably bring suffering. However,Christ supports all those who follow him along the
way of faithful and generous love.

Option Two

A reading from the first letter of St Peter   2:21-24
> Christ suffered for you,
> leaving you an example
> that you should follow in his steps.
> He committed no sin;
> no guile was found on his lips.
> When he was reviled,
> he did not revile in return.
> When he suffered,
> he did not threaten;
> but he trusted in him
> who judges justly.
> He himself bore our sins
> in his body on the tree,
> that we might die to sin
> and live to righteousness.
> This is the word of the Lord.

[Pause]

The road of suffering is narrow and difficult. It is a great comfort to us to know that Christ, the innocent and sinless one, has gone down this road before us, and gone down it to the end. This road is not the same since he travelled it. A bright light illuminates it.

Let us, therefore, walk along this road with courage and hope, knowing that though it leads to Calvary it does not end there but at Easter.

Option Three

A reading from the letter of St Paul to the Romans   8:31-32,35,37
> With God on our side who can be against us?
> Since God did not spare his own Son,
> but gave him up to benefit us all,
> we may be certain, after such a gift,
> that he will not refuse anything he can give.
> Christ not only died for us,

he rose from the dead,
and stands at God's right hand
pleading for us.
Nothing therefore can come between us and the love of
Christ,
even if we are troubled or worried,
or being persecuted,
or lacking food or clothes,
or being threatened or even attacked.
These are the trials through which we triumph,
by the power of him who loved us.
This is the word of the Lord.

[Pause]

If we have a hard life we should not think that God has abandoned us. Rather, we should feel a certain sense of privilege. This is the road Christ himself took, the 'narrow road' that brought him to Calvary. But it did not end there. It led to Easter.

Christ supports all those who follow him down this narrow road and shares his Easter victory with them.

First Station

JESUS IS CONDEMNED TO DEATH

'Pilate handed Jesus over to them to be crucified' (Jn 19:16).

First Approach

Jesus was condemned to death. He had his most basic right – the right to life – taken away from him. They decided to kill the one who came to bring us the fullness of life, the doctor who came to heal our wounds.

Before signing the death warrant, Pilate washed his hands – as if that exonerated him. And no doubt he slept well in his warm bed that night while Jesus slept in a cold tomb.

Having passed the death sentence on him, Pilate handed him over to his enemies. He was handed over to torturers who not only inflicted pain but mocked as well.

Everything was now out of his control. He was a helpless, powerless victim. They could push him around and do with him what they pleased. And they did.

To suffer when one is guilty is bad, but to suffer when one is innocent is worse. One's belief in fairness and justice is trampled into the dust. The fact that Jesus was a compassionate, sensitive person meant that he would have suffered more not less than others.

[Pause]

Second Approach

Jesus was a gentle, caring person. The Gospel tells us that 'he went about doing good'. How then did he come to be sentenced to death?

Jesus was indeed a kind and gentle person. But this does not mean that he was weak. He was a strong, assertive person. He stood up to the Scribes and Pharisees. He exposed their hypocrisy, calling them 'blind guides' and 'white-washed tombs'. If only he had used more temperate language.

Then there was his message. He spoke the truth in plain, unambiguous language. His words shocked some and infuriated others. His message caused disruption and division. It was a powerful message, a piercing light that came as a blessing to those intent on good but as a curse to those intent on evil. If only he had limited himself to saying nice things.

Furthermore, he insisted not only in associating with, but actually befriending, outcasts – sinners, lepers, Samaritans, and even members of the army of occupation (Roman soldiers). If only he had associated merely with deserving people.

Jesus said, 'Blessed are those who suffer in the cause of right.' He was the supreme example of this himself.

[Pause]

'What is the most precious thing in all the world? It is the consciousness of not participating in injustice' (Solzhenitsyn).

Prayers

For those who are on death row and for the terminally ill.

Lord, hear us.

Response: Lord, graciously hear us.

For those who are suffering in the cause of right.

Lord, hear us.

Response: Lord, graciously hear us.

OR

For the many summary executions which are carried out today in different parts of the world by government forces and by terrorists.

Lord, have mercy.

Response: Lord, have mercy.

For the little ones who have the death sentence passed on them even before they see the light of day.

Christ, have mercy.

Response: Christ, have mercy.

Psalm

Ps 54:5-8,23

Response: O God, listen to my prayer.

My heart is stricken within me,
death's terror is on me,
trembling and fear fall upon me
and horror overwhelms me. **R**

O that I had wings like a dove
to fly away and be at rest.
So I would escape far away
and take refuge in the desert. **R**

Entrust your cares to the Lord
and he will support you.
He will never allow
the just one to stumble. **R**

Reflection

THE BADNESS OF GOOD PEOPLE

When we look at the people who were responsible
for the death of Christ, what do we find?
We find that they were not a supremely
evil bunch of people, nor were they acting
out of the vilest possible motives.
In similar circumstances any of us
would probably have done the same,
because dark evil sleeps in us all.
But what does surprise us about them
is the fact that, apart from the Romans,
all were religious people.

It has been said of some religious people
that they have enough religion in them to hate
but not enough to love.

Second Station

JESUS TAKES UP HIS CROSS

In those days the condemned person was not put to death quickly and privately, but slowly and publicly. The aim was to discredit the person in the eyes of the people, and if possible to destroy his soul as well as his body.

Hence, Jesus was made to carry his cross through the streets of Jerusalem to the place of execution. Many who saw him, and who knew nothing about him, would have presumed that he was getting what he deserved, and would unthinkingly have joined in the public humiliation of him.

Jesus took up his cross. What we have to do is take up our cross. Our cross is made not of wood but of our burdens – worries, problems, illnesses. Maybe there is no big one but only a multiplicity of little ones. However, enough drops eventually fill the cup to overflowing.

The cross we carry may not even be visible to others. It may not be an outward thing but an inward thing – depression, grief … These can be cruel and heavy crosses even though we cannot weigh them on a scales.

The most painful cross of all, however, is the one over which we have no control, and in which we have no choice – the cross of living with a difficult person. It is a lot easier to choose a cross for ourselves than to accept the one that comes in the course of duty.

There is only one thing that can lighten such a cross. This one thing is love. Without love sacrifice is a heavy burden.

[Pause]

'To humiliate someone in public is to shed his blood' (Talmud).

Prayers

We all have some cross to carry; for the courage and strength to carry this cross.

Lord, hear us.

If there is some thing we have been shirking because we know it will cause us pain: that we may be able to face up to it.
Lord, hear us.

Psalm

Ps 27:1,3,13-14

Response: The Lord is my light and my help.

The Lord is my light and my help;
whom shall I fear?
The Lord is the stronghold of my life;
before whom shall I shrink? **R**

Though an army encamp against me
my heart would not fear.
Though war break out against me
even then would I trust. **R**

I am sure I shall see the Lord's goodness
in the land of the living.
Hope in him, hold firm and take heart.
Hope in the Lord. **R**

Reflection

PEOPLE ARE DIFFERENT

Some materials, such as copper,
disimprove when maltreated.
If you beat copper,
its crystals grow and it becomes
hard, taut, hostile.

Other materials, such as leather and felt,
improve when maltreated.
Iron is another example;
if you beat it, it rids itself of the dross
and becomes strong.

People are not all the same.
In the face of suffering

they behave differently.
Suffering hardens and embitters some;
whereas it softens others,
and makes them more compassionate.

Third Station

JESUS FALLS THE FIRST TIME

Jesus was getting weaker and weaker through loss of blood, lack of food and sleep, and as a result of the beating he had received. On top of all this there was the weight of the cross on his shoulders. It was getting heavier as he went along.

So he began to stumble, to wobble, to totter. The fall was inevitable. It was clear for all to see. Even so, no one raised a hand to prevent it. Finally his feet gave way under him and he fell.

Any kind of fall is damaging for one's morale. But a public fall is especially damaging. It is humbling to have one's weakness put on display. One feels that everybody is looking at you and talking about you.

Jesus was given little chance to regain his strength. The rough hands of the soldiers grabbed him and hauled him back onto his feet. He steadied himself for a second or two, then went on.

Many people today are weighed down by the burdens of life — poverty, sickness, unemployment, debts ... Everything adds up and accumulates until they reach a point where they just cannot cope any longer. And so they fall. In the fall, their already meagre self-worth and dignity take a crushing blow.

To all such people Jesus says, 'Come to me, all you who labour and are overburdened, and I will give you rest.'

[Pause]

'I don't like people who have never fallen or stumbled' (Boris Pasternak).

Prayers

For those who have fallen under their burden of problems and worries: that they may be able to rise again.

Lord, hear us.

That we may have an eye for those who are overburdened, and give them a helping hand.

Lord, hear us.

Psalm
Ps 25:1-3,15-16,20-21

Response: To you, O Lord, I lift up my soul.

> To you, O Lord, I lift up my soul.
> I trust you, let me not be disappointed;
> do not let my enemies triumph.
> Those who hope in you shall not be disappointed. **R**
>
> My eyes are always on the Lord;
> for he rescues my feet from the snare.
> Turn to me and have mercy
> for I am lonely and poor. **R**
>
> Preserve my life and rescue me.
> Do not disappoint me, you are my refuge.
> May innocence and uprightness protect me,
> for my hope is in you, O Lord. **R**

Reflection

INDIFFERENCE

> A large crowd followed him along the way.
> Some of these were hostile towards him.
> Some were merely curious.
> And some were indifferent.
> Indifference is the real danger.
> It is the worst of all.
>
> Speaking of the Holocaust, Elie Wiesel said:
> 'The victims suffered more,
> and more profoundly,
> from the indifference of the onlookers
> than from the brutality of the executioners.'
>
> The opposite to love is not hate but indifference,
> and indifference is the greatest evil in the world.

Fourth Station

JESUS MEETS HIS MOTHER

This was a very painful meeting – painful for Mary and also for Jesus. What made it so painful was the love they had for one another. If there was no love, there would have been no bond, and therefore no pain.

But the pain for Mary must have been excruciating – to see her Son condemned to death and now being made a spectacle in public. What made it even harder for her was the fact that she probably did not understand why her Son had come to this sorry state. If only she could understand that it was truly unavoidable, that there was no other way, it would have been a little easier.

Nevertheless, she did not abandon him. As his mother, she went on believing in him and loving him. The Bible uses a mother's love for her child as an image of God's love for us. 'Does a woman forget her baby at the breast, or fail to cherish the son of her womb? Yet even if these forget, I will never forget you' (Is 49:15).

Mary's pain added to the pain of Jesus. People do not like to bring sorrow to those they love. Jesus saw her pain and knew that his plight was the cause of it. Yet he could do nothing about it.

And yet, in spite of everything, the meeting with his mother was a comfort to him. They would not meet again until the end.

[Pause]

'Do people weigh you down? Do not carry them on your shoulder. Take them into your heart' (Helder Camara).

Prayers

For parents who are suffering because of their children: e.g., those who are caught up in the horror of drug addiction.

Lord, hear us.

That Mary, our spiritual mother, may help us to follow the footsteps of Jesus especially when the going gets rough.

Lord, hear us.

Psalm

Ps 139:7-10,13-14

Response: O Lord, you search me and you know me.

> Lord, where can I go from your spirit,
> or where can I flee from your face?
> If I climb the heavens, you are there.
> If I lie in the grave, you are there. **R**
>
> If I take the wings of the dawn
> and dwell at the sea's furthest end,
> even there your hand would lead me,
> your right hand would hold me fast. **R**
>
> For it was you who created my being,
> knit me together in my mother's womb.
> I thank you for the wonder of my being,
> for the wonders of all your creation. **R**

Reflection

PARENTS AND CHILDREN

> Children are like kites.
> Parents spend half a lifetime
> trying to get them off the ground.
> And what happens?
> They have hardly succeeded
> when the lifeline snaps,
> and the kites soar, alone and free.
>
> Parents have nothing to give their children,
> only a duty to open them to their own lives.
> When the children are old enough
> to take responsibility for those lives,
> the parents must be prepared to let them go;
> they must allow them to live their own lives
> according to their own lights.
>
> To let someone we love go entirely free,
> is the most difficult thing in the world.

Fifth Station

SIMON OF CYRENE HELPS JESUS
TO CARRY HIS CROSS

'As they were leading them away they seized a man, Simon from Cyrene, who was coming in from the country, and made him shoulder the cross and carry it behind Jesus' (Lk 23:26).

It is clear from this that Simon was not a volunteer but a conscript. The soldiers forced him to help Jesus with his cross. It is highly unlikely that he relished the task. To be associated with a condemned man was not something one would relish. Even at the best of times, the burden of another is twice as heavy as our own burden.

It is also very unlikely that he knew the true identity of the man he was helping. We do not know how it affected him. Did he, for instance, keep his distance from Jesus? Or did he allow himself to feel and show compassion for him? It is possible to help while keeping an icy detachment from the person we help.

As for Jesus, he must have wondered where his friends were. Was there no one to lend a hand but this stranger. Nevertheless, he accepted Simon's help, and no doubt was grateful for it. To see a fellow human being beside you makes the world seem a more friendly place. Who knows but a bond will form, and a comrade-ship will develop? In bearing our burdens we must not be too proud to accept the help of others. It is a mistake to think that we can make it on our own.

When someone is at the end of his strength, lend him the support of yours, and see what wonders that can work. Besides, when you do this you are doing what Simon did. 'As long as you did it to one of these, you did it to me,' says the Lord.

[Pause]

'The person who does a good deed is instantly ennobled' (Emerson).

Prayers

For those who are alone, and who have no one to help them when they fall.
Lord, hear us.
For those who have helped us to carry our burdens.
Lord, hear us.

Psalm   Ps 56:2-3,6-7,9-10

Response: Have mercy on me, O God.

> Have mercy on me, God, foes crush me;
> they fight me all day long and oppress me.
> My foes crush me all the day long,
> for many fight proudly against me. **R**

> All day long they distort my words,
> all their thought is to harm me.
> They band together in ambush,
> track me down and seek my life. **R**

> You, Lord, have kept an account of my wanderings;
> you have kept a record of my tears.
> My foes will be put to flight
> on the day that I call on you. **R**

Reflection

> Simon took the cross from Jesus
> and carried it for him.
> Most times we cannot do this.
> We cannot remove the illness or pain
> another person is suffering,
> and take it on ourselves.
> We cannot suffer in that person's place.

> What then can we do?
> We can stand beside those who are suffering,
> supporting and encouraging them,
> so that they find the courage and strength
> to carry their own cross.

Sixth Station

VERONICA WIPES THE FACE OF JESUS

A woman called Veronica stepped out of the crowd that lined the road, and with a towel wiped the dust, sweat, and blood from the face of Jesus. It called for a lot of courage to help someone who was the object of public derision.

It was not a prudent thing to be seen to associate with or give succour to a condemned person. Yet she did so in the full glare of the soldiers, thereby risking a lash from one of their whips.

Unlike Simon, Veronica was a volunteer. Her's was a spontaneous act of kindness. It is good to give when asked, but it is better to give unasked, through understanding.

Why did she do it? Because she was that kind of person. The kind who cannot see another person in pain and stand idly by. The kind who feels compelled to do something, however, small, for the suffering person.

No doubt there were others who felt sympathy for Jesus and who would have liked to help him. What prevented them from doing so? Fear and cowardice. Veronica alone translated her sympathy into deeds.

There is a tradition that she brought away the imprint of the face of Jesus on the towel. we cannot be sure of this. But what we can be sure of is that she brought the face of Jesus with her. Every act of compassion reveals the face of Jesus.

There can be little doubt but that her simple, but brave gesture, meant a great deal to Jesus.

[Pause]

'There is no more important thing in life than compassion for a fellow human being" (Tolstoy).

Prayers

For those who wipe the faces of the sick, especially mothers and nurses.

Lord, hear us.

That we may not be afraid to help another person even if it is not a popular thing to do. Lord, hear us.

OR

For the cowardice that prevents us from acting.
Lord, have mercy.
For the times we felt sympathy for someone in pain or need, yet did nothing to help them.
Christ, have mercy.

Psalm

Ps 34:8-9,18-21

Response: Taste and see that the Lord is good.

The angel of the Lord is encamped
around those who revere him, to rescue them.
Taste and see that the Lord is good.
They are happy who seek refuge in him. **R**

The just call and the Lord hears
and rescues them in all their distress.
The Lord is close to the broken-hearted;
those whose spirit is crushed he will save. **R**

Many are the trials of the upright
but the Lord will come to rescue them
He will keep guard over all their bones,
not one of their bones shall be broken. **R**

Reflection

A CUP OF COLD WATER

What Veronica did for Jesus
was in itself a very small thing.
Often what we can do for someone in pain
may seem to us to be very trivial:
to offer a word of encouragement or of sympathy,
to write a few lines, to send some flowers,
to bake a cake, or just to drop in for a minute.
But this should not cause us
to neglect or underestimate it.

Sixth Station

In certain circumstances a simple gesture
transcends itself and takes on an importance
far beyond its actual value.
As simple a thing as a cup of cold water
can save a person from death in the desert.

Seventh Station

JESUS FALLS A SECOND TIME

Simon's help provided Jesus with a respite from his burden. So too did Veronica's gesture of compassion. But, alas, the respite was all too brief.

The weakness came on again. He struggled against it. He tried desperately to keep on putting one foot in front of the other. But it was no good. Her started to get dizzy. Before he knew it he was on the ground again.

Once again he got no sympathy. He was not even allowed a minute to rest. The soldiers felt he was making things difficult for them. So they dragged him to his feet, shouted at him, and forced him to go on.

Today there are lots of people for whom life is very cruel. Many of them feel that no one understands them or cares about them.

Think of the victims of alcoholism and drug addiction who, no matter how hard they try, fall again and again. Think also of the families that are dragged down with them.

Think of the victims of desertion – wives and husbands. With the best will in the world, at times life becomes too much for them, and they collapse into a pit of depression.

Think of abandoned or neglected children for whom life will forever be a hard, uphill struggle.

Think of those for whom life is an unrelenting battle against grinding hardship.

[Pause]

'A stone is not a human being, and even stones get crushed' (Solzhenitsyn).

Prayers

For those who have suffered a nervous breakdown; for those who are struggling to rise from alcoholism or drug addiction.
Lord, hear us.
That in our struggles we may not be too proud to ask for help.
Lord, hear us.

Psalm

Ps 130:5-8,1-2

Response: Out of the depths I cry to you, O Lord.

My soul is waiting for the Lord,
I count on his word.
My soul is longing for the Lord
more than watchman for daybreak. **R**

Because with the Lord there is mercy
and fullness of redemption,
Israel indeed he will redeem
from all its iniquity. **R**

Out of the depths I cry to you, O Lord,
Lord, hear my voice.
O let your ears be attentive
to the voice of my pleading. **R**

Reflection

HUMAN WARMTH
The one thing the sufferer longs for,
and which we all can give,
is human warmth.

Kindness and human sympathy
are often more important than any medicine.
People are ready to forget any torments
for one kind word.

'The care of a patient,
the welcome given to a fugitive,
forgiveness itself,
are only worthwhile
because of the smile that goes with them.'

Antoine de Saint Exupery

Eighth Station

SOME WOMEN OF JERUSALEM WEEP FOR JESUS

'Large numbers of people followed him, and of women too, who mourned and lamented for him. But Jesus turned to them and said. "Daughters of Jerusalem, do not weep for me; weep rather for yourselves and for your children."' (Lk 23:27-28).

Certain noblewomen used to try to give a little comfort to condemned criminals by offering them soothing drinks. The women in question may have belonged to this class.

They did not hide their sympathy behind stony faces. They were not afraid to let Jesus see that they cared about him.

If we care about others we should not be afraid to let them know this.

Jesus was not being dismissive of their sympathy. Quite the contrary. He accepted it and returned it.

He knew that Jerusalem would soon know days of terror. It would be razed to the ground. Its inhabitants, especially women and children, would suffer enormously.

He was forewarning the women and showing compassion for them in advance. It was as it he was saying to them, 'My suffering is nothing compared to what yours will be.'

It says volumes about the kind of person Jesus was that from the depths of his own pain and humiliation he could feel for the plight of those women and offer them comfort.

One's pain can so easily turn into rage, so that one sees nothing, and wants only to lash out blindly at whoever happens to be within range.

[Pause]

'No one can fight the night alone and hope to conquer it' (Elie Wiesel).

Prayers

That we may weep for our own sins before considering the sins of others.

Lord, hear us.

STATIONS OF THE CROSS

That our own experiences of suffering may make us compassionate towards others who suffer.

Lord, hear us.

Psalm

Ps 52:3-6,12-13

Response: Have mercy on me, God, in your kindness.

Have mercy on me, God, in your kindness.
In your compassion blot out my offence.
O wash me more and more from my guilt
and cleanse me from my sin. **R**

My offences truly I know them;
my sin is always before me.
Against you, you alone, have I sinned;
what is evil in your sight I have done. **R**

A pure heart create for me, O God,
put a steadfast spirit within me.
Do not cast me away from your presence,
nor deprive me of your holy spirit. **R**

Reflection

LET THEM KNOW

'It is no good caring deeply for people
and concealing this behind
a barrier of icy professionalism.
If people do not know themselves cared for,
they will be a prey to a thousand fears
of being misunderstood or rejected.'
Sheila Cassidy

Jesus wept openly at the death of Lazarus.
Some people, however, are ashamed of tears.
They see them as a sign of weakness.
Tears are in fact a kind of riches.
They show that we have feelings,

that we can be moved to compassion.
In short, that we have a heart.

The heart of one person holds inexhaustible
riches for the heart of another person.

Ninth Station

JESUS FALLS A THIRD TIME

Jesus was now absolutely drained of strength. He was totally exhausted. He began to totter once more. And so he fell yet again. He was reduced to a sorry state. Each fall was more painful than the preceding one. And each time it got harder to recover.

Left to himself he probably would not have made it. But Calvary was now in sight. They dragged him to his feet, and somehow he made it to the place of execution.

How many people today are reduced to this sorry state, and are perhaps in some ways worse off than Jesus was. They feel utterly helpless and hopeless.

They are physically and mentally exhausted. Their well of energy and strength has run dry. They have no will, no spirit left to carry on.

They see nothing ahead of them but pain. They are in a state of despair. The feel alienated from themselves, from others and even from God.

Think of alcoholics and addicts who have reached that most painful and humbling state known as "rock bottom".

Think of those children who have been abused, and who are in a pit of guilt and shame from which they find it impossible to rise.

Think of the desperately poor who have to live on scraps from the table of the well-off, and who are always down in the dumps.

[Pause]

'A man with a grain of faith in God never loses hope, because he ever believes in the ultimate triumph of truth' (Gandhi).

Prayers

For down-and-out, broken, lost, and deeply wounded people.
Lord, hear us.
For those who are on the edge of despair and suicide.
Lord, hear us.

Psalm

Ps 142:2-3,6-8

Response: With all my voice I cry to the Lord.

With all my voice I cry to the Lord,
with all my voice I entreat the Lord.
I pour out my trouble before him;
I tell him all my distress. **R**

I cry to you, O lord.
I have said: 'You are my refuge,
all I have left in the land of the living.'
Listen then to my cry
for I am in the depths of distress. **R**

Rescue me from those who pursue me
for they are stronger than I.
Bring my soul out of this prison
and then I shall praise your name. **R**

Reflection

KEEPING UP ONE'S SPIRIT

In times of trial and suffering
to keep up one's spirit is essential.
The spirit is our greatest source of strength.
When we lose it we pine away
like a tree whose roots have been cut.

However, the spirit is very fragile.
It is easily damaged, easily broken.
And just as the body needs nourishment
so too does the spirit.
On what does one nourish the spirit?
On such things as meaning, hope, love,
prayer, and faith in God.

Tenth Station

JESUS IS STRIPPED OF HIS CLOTHES

On reaching the pace of execution Jesus was stripped of his clothes. The main aim of this was to further degrade and humiliate the condemned person. To be naked is also to be totally vulnerable.

Jesus now had nothing. Everything had been taken away from him. Those who lose everything frequently lose themselves too. Not so Jesus. He did not forget who he was, and maintained his dignity to the end.

The soldiers divided his clothes among them, casting lots to see who would have his robe.

In Auschwitz and the other death camps, the SS collected the boots, shoes, clothes, jewellery, gold fillings, and even the hair of their victims.

Spare a thought for those today who are stripped of elementary human rights.

For those who are stripped of the bare necessities of life – food, clothes, shelter ...

For children who, stripped of love and care, become victims of neglect and exploitation.

For old people who, stripped of companionship, become victims of loneliness.

For those who never get any recognition or appreciation and so are stripped of self-worth.

[Pause]

'Shame is imputed not to the one who suffers it but to the one who inflicts it' (St Francis of Assisi).

Prayers

For those who have been stripped of their dignity and self-worth. Lord, hear us.

That we may realise that we cannot degrade another person without degrading ourselves. Lord, hear us.

Psalm

Ps 31:2-6

Response: Into your hands I commend my spirit.

In you, O Lord, I take refuge.
Let me never be put to shame.
In your justice, set me free,
hear me and speedily rescue me. **R**

Be a rock of refuge for me,
a mighty stronghold to save me,
for you are my rock, my stronghold. **R**

For your name's sake, lead me and guide me.
Release me from the snares they have hidden
for you are my refuge, Lord. **R**

Into your hands I commend my spirit.
It is you who will redeem me, Lord. **R**

Reflection

STRIPPED

While in Auschwitz, Primo Levi suffered the indignity of being
stripped countless times. Of the experience he has this to say:

'A naked man feels that all his nerves
and tendons are severed.
He is a helpless prey
Clothes, even the foul clothes which were distributed,
even the crude clogs with their wooden soles,
are a tenuous but indispensable defence.
Anyone who does not have them
no longer perceives himself as a human being,
but rather a worm;
naked, slow, ignoble, prone on the ground.
He knows that he can be crushed at any moment.'

The Drowned and the Saved, p.90.

Eleventh Station

JESUS IS NAILED TO THE CROSS

Jesus was nailed to the cross. He hung there, unable to move hand or foot, He was utterly powerless.

This was the point of no return. Up to now the condemned person might have thought, 'Perhaps this is a bad dream? Perhaps it is some kind of rough play-acting?'

In other words, there existed the faint possibility of a reprieve, at least in the mind of the condemned, especially in the mind of one who, like Jesus, was totally innocent. Something would happen. Someone would intervene. God himself even?

But with the nailing to the cross this tiny flicker of hope was cruelly extinguished. The stark truth struck home. This was for real, and there would be no reprieve.

The soldiers had their orders. They did not consider it their business to question the morality of those orders. Their job was to carry them out exactly. This they did. They were not noted for their gentleness.

The awfulness of it, the excruciating pain it involved, is beyond imagining. Yet Jesus refused the drugged wine which was offered and which might have deadened that pain. He insisted on living his death.

He was crucified between two thieves. No doubt his enemies reckoned these were fitting company for him. Indeed they were. They were exactly the kind he would have wanted, for he said, 'I came to seek out and to save the lost.'

And he did succeed in saving one of them.

[Pause]

A person without fear is no hero; the person who overcomes fear is' (Solzhenitsyn).

Prayers
For the severely handicapped and those who are paralysed.
Lord, hear us.

For members of the security forces – that they may never violate their conscience.
Lord, hear us.
For prisoners – that they may not lose hope.
Lord, hear us.

Psalm

Ps 42:2,4, 12

Response: My soul is thirsting for God,
the God of my life.

Like a deer that yearns
for running streams,
so my soul is yearning
for you, my God. **R**

My tears have become my bread,
by night, by day,
as I hear it said all the day long:
'Where is your God?' **R**

Why are you cast down, my soul,
why groan within me?
Hope in God; I will praise him still,
my saviour and my God. **R**

Reflection

IN GOD'S ARMS

Etty Hillesum was a young Jewish woman who died in Auschwitz in 1943. Here is an extract from her diary.

'I don't feel in anybody's clutches;
I feel safe in God's arms,
and no matter whether I am sitting
at this beloved old desk now,
or in a bare room in the Jewish district,
or perhaps in a labour camp
under SS guards in a month's time –
I shall always feel safe in God's arms.'

Twelfth Station

JESUS DIES ON THE CROSS

'Near the cross of Jesus stood his mother and his mother's sister, Mary the wife of Clopas, Mary of Magdala ... and the disciple Jesus loved' (Jn 19:25-26).

First Approach

They stood there. If only they could do something for Jesus, it would have been easier for them. But there was nothing.

It is terrible to be beside a friend who is suffering (or dying), and know there is nothing you can do. It makes you feel useless and inadequate. You desperately want to run away.

Often there is even nothing you can say. For words too have become impossible.

In which case, our only ministry is one of simple presence.

Even though this is difficult, it is a precious and vital thing. Like Mary, we must stay with the suffering or dying person. A reassuring, supportive presence can mean the world to the sufferer.

To know that there is someone there who cares, makes the world of difference. It saves him/her from the awful prospect of dying alone and abandoned.

In spite of the presence of these few friends, Jesus died in darkness, taunted and jeered by his enemies.

Nevertheless, he died abandoning himself into the hands of his heavenly Father.

In the face of death, only God can save us.
[Pause]

Second Approach

Nobody likes to die. People fear death. They cling to life, even when it is not great.

Jesus was no exception. He too wanted to live. In the garden he prayed that God might save him from this hour of pain and shame.

But once he saw that there was no other way, he did not run

away. He faced death. And the dignity with which he died made a big impression on at least two of those present – the thief and the centurion.

Even though he was the victim of a terrible injustice and awful ill-treatment, he died without bitterness. He forgave those who were responsible for his death.

Even from the depths of his own pain he still managed to care for others. He brought hope to the good thief. He thought about his mother and asked John to look after her.

'Some people are like sugar-cane, even when crushed in the mill, completely squashed, reduced to pulp, all they yield is sweetness' (Helder Camara).

He died praying. His last words were a prayer of abandonment to God: 'Father, into your hands I entrust my spirit.'

Then he dropped his head and died. It was as simple as that. One minute he was talking. Next minute he was silent.

One dies as one has lived. One does not suddenly become a hero or a saint in death.

Having taught us how to live, Jesus also taught us how to die. [Pause]

'When your last hour strikes count only on what you have become' (Antoine de Saint Exupery).

Prayers

That we may be able to forgive all those who have harmed us in any way. Lord, hear us.

For the dying and all those who minister to them.
Lord, hear us.

Psalm   Ps 22:2-5,7-9,11,12
Response: My God, my God, why have you forsaken me?

> My God, my God, why have you forsaken me?
> You are far from my plea and the cry of my distress.
> O my God, I call by day and you give no reply;
> I call by night and I find no peace. **R**

Yet you, O God, are holy,
enthroned on the praises of Israel.
In you our fathers put their trust;
they trusted and you set them free. **R**

But I am the laughing-stock of the people.
They curl their lips, they toss their heads.
'He trusted in the Lord, let him save him;
let him release him if this is his friend.' **R**

To you I was committed from my birth,
from my mother's womb you have been my God.
Do not leave me alone in my distress;
come close, there is none else to help. **R**

Reflection

THE SILENCE OF GOD

We wonder at the silence of God
in the face of the death of the innocent.
Why does he not intervene,
or at least say something?

Yet when a disaster happens,
and a whole stadium full of people
observe a minute's silence,
what a powerful statement that silence makes.

Everything stops, no one moves,
a hush falls over the crowd,
not even a whisper is heard ...

Before the mystery of death
words are not only inadequate but impossible.
Silence seems the only true and proper response.

Thirteenth Station

JESUS' BODY IS TAKEN DOWN
FROM THE CROSS

Jesus was dead. Even though the evidence was staring his friends in the face, the reality had not yet sunk in. Nor could it. It was too early. Besides, there were things to be done.

The first thing that had to be done was to take down his body from the cross. To do this they had to get permission from the authorities, because his death had to be certified. Only then were they allowed to claim his body.

And so it was taken down from the cross, and his mother took it into her arms. It was in a sad state – puffy, dirty, sweat-stained, blood-stained, bruised from falls and blows, lacerated from the whip lashes, nails and spear.

The sorrow for his friends was no doubt immense. But for Mary it must have been absolutely overwhelming. Parents do not expect their children to die before them. And this was not even an ordinary death. This was a violent, shameful death.

Mercifully his body was at least in one piece. Spare a thought for the relatives of those who are victims of road accidents, violence, terrorism, war ... bodies are frequently so badly mutilated that the next of kin are not always able to recognise their loved ones.

Spare a thought too for those who in dealing with such bodies have to endure gruesome sights and experiences – doctors, nurses, police, pathologists, ambulance and fire personnel ...

[Pause]

'Of what use is a compassion that does not take its object into its arms?' (Antoine de Saint Exupery).

Prayers

For first-aid personnel, and for all those who deal with the victims of violence. Lord, hear us.

For those who work in the emergency rooms of hospitals. Lord, hear us.

Psalm

Ps 115:10-15

Response: Precious in the eyes of the Lord
      is the death of his faithful.

> I trusted, even when I said:
> 'I am sorely afflicted,'
> and when I said in my alarm:
> 'There is no one I can trust.' **R**

> How can I repay the Lord
> for his goodness to me?
> The cup of salvation I will raise;
> I will call on the Lord's name. **R**

> My vows to the Lord I will fulfil
> before all his people.
> O precious in the eyes of the Lord
> is the death of his faithful. **R**

Reflection

THE WOUNDS OF LOVE

> Those who love others pick up
> a lot of wounds in the course of life.
> Perhaps there are no great ones,
> no nail marks or spear wounds,
> only a multiplicity of little ones –
> a host of scratches, wrinkles, welts.

> To these we must add the invisible ones:
> the furrows left on the mind
> by fears, worries, and anxieties;
> the bruises left on the heart
> by disappointments and ingratitude.

> But all these are honourable wounds.
> They are the proofs of love.

Fourteenth Station

JESUS IS BURIED

Now that the body had been taken down from the cross, they had to decide what to do with it. The bodies of executed men were seldom buried. They were normally left out in the open to be eaten by the vultures. But the friends of Jesus saw to it that this would not happen to his body.

They decided to bury it. But where? It was then that a devout and good man, Joseph of Arimathea, came along with the offer of a tomb made from stone in a nearby garden.

It was a Jewish custom to wrap the bodies of the dead in linen cloths and also to put sweet spices between the folds of the cloths. It was Nicodemus, the same man who came to Jesus by night, who provided the cloths and spices.

They wrapped the body in the linen cloths and placed it in the tomb. It was not the kind of farewell they wanted to say. Everything had to be done quickly because the Sabbath rest began at six o'clock. Having rolled a large stone across the mouth of the tomb, they went away.

Darkness fell, Silence wrapped itself around them. They felt numb and empty. A terrible truth began to sink in. He was gone, and it seemed forever. And so they began to grieve.

But at least they had the consolation of giving Jesus a burial. Spare a thought for those who do not even have the consolation of a burial because the bodies of their loved ones are never found.

[Pause]

'Life is only a kind of sowing, the harvest is not here' (Van Gogh).

Prayers

For all the dead whose faith is known to God alone.
Lord, hear us.

For those who are grieving, and for those who are in a tomb of loneliness or depression. Lord, hear us.

Psalm

Ps 16:1-2,9-11

Response: Preserve me, God, I take refuge in you.

> Preserve me, God, I take refuge in you.
> I say to the Lord: 'You are my God.
> My happiness lies in you alone.' **R**
>
> And so my heart rejoices, my soul is glad;
> even my body shall rest in safety.
> For you will not leave my soul among the dead,
> nor let your beloved know decay. **R**
>
> You will show me the path of life,
> the fullness of joy in your presence,
> at your right hand happiness for ever. **R**

Reflection

> Lord,
> remember not only people of good will
> but also those of ill will.
> Do not remember only the sufferings
> that have been inflicted on us,
> but remember too the fruit we have bought
> as a result of this suffering:
> the comradeship and loyalty,
> the humility and courage,
> the generosity and greatness of heart
> that have grown out of it.
> And when they come to judgement,
> let all the fruits that we have borne
> be their forgiveness.

Prayer found in a concentration camp

Conclusion

We leave the story of Jesus here knowing, however, that we are omitting the most important part of it, namely, the resurrection. Good came from this evil, joy from this pain, victory from this defeat, glory from this shame, life from this death.
[Pause]

Let us pray
Thank you, Lord, for sharing our struggles, our pain, our fear of death, and even death itself. Be with us in our sufferings. May we who have followed your painful journey to Calvary, witness to you by lives of prayer, love, and service, and so come to share in your Easter victory. We ask this through you, who live and reign with the Father and the Holy Spirit, one God for ever and ever. Amen.

The Way of the Cross

Miriam Pollard

Introduction

We want to go some where. The Way of the Cross is a road, and roads are made to be walked on.

What have we come for?

We have come to ponder and to pray. The word 'station' means a place to stop, to stand still. The Stations of the Cross are places along the road where we can enter and accept a mystery we might otherwise be too busy, angry, or discouraged to consider.

The Way of the Cross is a special kind of prayer. It is a drama, Drama is not an artificial thing; a play is not a diversion from real life. A good play is more real than anything we are used to calling real. Drama turns life inside out to show us what it means. The walking and waiting that this prayer involves are part of the prayer, for they are part of the play.

We are not setting apart half an hour of our daily existence for a sacred purpose. We are bringing our daily existence home to its own explanation, and saying yes to what it really means. The Way of the Cross is our daily existence – interpreted, recognized, and accepted.

The particular beauty of this prayer is that we could not make it unless, in a sense, we had already finished it. For part of its meaning is that its ending has worked backward into its beginning, Easter into the Condemnation, and the garden of the Resurrection into our blighted Paradise. We are not walking in a wilderness, for Easter runs like a brook beside, across, and even under the road on which we travel.

First Station
THE TRIAL

Beginning can be difficult. We are scattered, for one thing, dry and disconnected by Ezekiel's field of bones. We would be glad enough to pick up the pieces and start out fresh, but we have never been able to manage it. Beginnings always seem to start in the wrong place, and we feel we have not had a chance to begin anything properly since the first day of school – maybe since the day we were born, and we are not altogether sure about that.

We are also worried. It is as if our problems would run away and get worse if they were not being constantly worried about. We can find ourselves at the Sixth Station without ever having got to the first.

Be glad it does not matter that much. Pick up one piece of yourself if that is all you can get your hands on – one worry, or sorrow, or ecstatic joy. One will do. Fit it slowly and deliberately into the accepting heart of Christ and let it go. He will take care of the rest of you.

We have to be on our way.

Second Station
ACCEPTING

The cross is not that thing you hate and cannot get rid of, that weight you pick up every morning and haul to the end of the day. The cross is not dead wood. You plant it and it grows. The shadow of the cross is not a fearful thing. Shade can be comforting.

The human heart has two great quarrels with itself – suffering and guilt. In the shadow the cross these two great adversaries sit down and make peace with us. Hot, sweaty, short-tempered and short-sighted, they come in out of the sun. The strident voices hush, the argument, the questioning.

To accept the cross is not to acquiesce in our own destruction or to let ourselves in for more of what we now cannot stand. It is to keep ourselves from looking at things all wrong and adding to the pain.

Let the cross root. Let it grow branches and be shade.

Third Station
THE FIRST FALL

This is not much of a start if we are going somewhere – to fall, to be crowded, to be yanked up and hustled off without a chance to think the matter over. You need some mental space in which to come to terms with what falling is about.

Or do you?

John Donne spoke of the Advent Christ as 'immensity … shut in a little room.' A lot of life is shut in little room – without adequate resources of time or thought, education or even love. We all have our personal litanies of constriction.

At this point in our travels, we can at least take notice that Donne's rhyme closes with the only appropriate word – 'womb.' We can agree that being shut in little room has something to do with being born.

Fourth Station
THE MOTHER

Letting go is part of responsibility and also of love. We can cling to one form of a relationship because we cannot imagine any other. But a moment comes when the bearer of our love walks off into another country of the spirit, perhaps a place of immanent destruction, and we do not know the geography. Some people have to reach their Easter without us. At least it can look that way at first.

There is something else we can cling to. We can nurse our regret at having to let go or at remembering that we did not and that in any number of ways we have botched the relationship. Who of us has not given the wrong advice or used other people to our own advantage instead of theirs or known ourselves inadequate to another's need? We have to let go of our regret, for this kind of self-torment is not contrition but despair.

There is a season, a season for everything under the sun. There is a way of cherishing which entrusts our loves to their own seasons of Resurrection.

Fifth Station
SIMON

We have been loved; we still are loved – inadequately perhaps, but people do the best they can. We have been helped, and maybe the love and the help would seem less inadequate if we stopped awhile to ponder the privilege of having them. We could take count of service and courtesy, kindness, humour, friendship and generosity.

The privilege of loving is just as good as the privilege of being loved. They go together. But giving does not mean forcing on others the things we want to give, in order to feel valuable. It means respect for what they really need. It can mean providing space for them to make mistakes in, or space for honesty on either hand.

Sixth Station
VERONICA

It does not happen this way to us. We wish it would; we would like to have the chance for such a graceful gesture; we would like to carry home the picture on a scarf. Something else happens to us. We are the scarf. It is only theory until one day it matters very much.

Do not think it is always easy to be yourself and someone else, to be yourself and also an other. We cannot get ourselves on order. There is this face inside that is ours and someone else's, and the form it takes is determined as much by what we are not as by what we are.

The face of Christ is being pressed into our capacity for human expansion, for love, service and joy; but also into our limitation, into the fabric of all we do not want to be, all we would rather transcend, change or ignore. The face of Christ looks out at us from a world of other people, from lives that attract and sustain us; and from lives we would rather transcend, change, or ignore.

Seventh Station

SECOND FALL

This.is a strange circumstance in which to celebrate the works of human skill. But we should. Falling down is not what we were born for. Falling is not only unavoidable but useful, even necessary. We should however praise the hands by which we are raised up, supported, and set once more on our way.

Let us praise the skills of human understanding which appreciate the value and potential of our falls and teach us how to walk again. But let us be glad as well for the medicine, art, and architecture, the farming and the books, the labour which fashions a thousand methods of lightening our burden.

Praise the marvel of the human tongue and all its languages; praise every gift in which God visits the world and places in our hands something of his own power and concern.

Eighth Station

THE MOURNING WOMEN

'Mourn for yourselves and for your children.'
Yes, but let the Resurrection in.

We are torn.We know it is not right to let the sorrow of the world, its malice, violence, and exploitation paralyse our capacity to help. The magnitude of all that is wrong is enough to numb the healing will. But it must not. Despair is not compassion. What limited but practical help can we give – today, tomorrow, and another tomorrow?

On the other hand, we have to settle for a lot less than we want. The world will not permit itself to be made over to our specifications. We ought not to be so compelled by our own vision of improvement that everyone in reach suffers as much from our ministrations as from the original disorder.

Ninth Station
THIRD FALL

It is strange how running can feel so much like falling down. Some of us like to do too much. It is a kind of importance; it is better than being ignored. Some of us do not like it at all. We do not like always feeling that there is something we forgot. We would like to pray and be wholly there, to get to the end of a day in one piece instead of two dozen, to finish one task at a time, pay attention to one person at a time.

We try to keep our balance, and get mad because our trying is so pitiful and unsuccessful. We are angry at our anger and terribly afraid of getting lost in our desperation.

Bring it here – the frazzle, the failure and the anger. Hand him the desperation, Be still for just one minute. God fell down; he knows all about it. He brushes the tips of his fingers over the jagged edges of our fractured hearts.

Tenth Station
STRIPPING

What we can do and give and be for others is only part of love. If you add what they can do and give and be for us, you still do not have the whole of it.

Sometimes we have to let things be taken away, and not only things but our own selves. The occasion might be small. An opinion, a conviction, a cultural outlook may not be shared or confirmed by someone else. The outlook is more than a garment: it is a second skin, and in its rejection, we ourselves go unconfirmed.

The occasion may be vast beyond reckoning, as deep as bereavement, as radical as exile or abandonment.We do not belong; sometimes it feels as if we do not exist.

But belonging is something inward which no one can take away. Someday we will know this, and we will know that only from this place of belonging can we truly love.

Eleventh Station
NAILING

If we are going somewhere, what are the nails for? This is not a pause along the way; it is a full stop.

A lot of life can feel this way. The gift of responsibility can upon occasion feel this way, the commitment given in a gentler hour. 'I did not know. I never thought'. Of course not. That is the point. The point holds when we want to run away, when we are in danger of skipping out on the dark sweet mystery of the responsible choice.

The nail holds. It also pierces – down to a region of the heart whose entrance would be locked except for promises, promises made before we knew what they would expect of us. This is a place of beautiful secrets told only in the dark, a place where the waters of Easter flow very close and clear.

Twelfth Station

DEATH

We are climbing now. The road gets wider here, for everyone is coming. The brook too swells, as if the closer we come to its source, the wider it grows. Somewhere near here it begins, and we would find the place if only we could see. Why has the sun gone out?

Darkness is a silence of the heart. It erases the non-essential. We sit in a circle listening with our eyes, our ears, and our hearts. What we want to do and be and become – those terribly important concerns which cluttered up the outset of our journey – settle themselves over there on the fringe of the crowd. We sit in the dark at the centre and listen to the breathing of God.

Thirteenth Station

RECEIVING THE BODY

It was always other people – other people whose children went to prison or who were too poor to feed them right. Or maybe it was not; maybe it was always us.

But we know now, some way, what it is like to be unable to provide, unable to stop harm. Or we know what it is like to be the one in jail or the one who in some other way, has no more life to live. It is over.

Or has it just begun? This quietude, this cessation of the struggle with appearances because there are not any left to struggle with, this evaporation of alternatives – is it a place of creation? It cannot be unless – unless God has been here before us and is still here; unless this negation is the unbinding of his wings, a night rocked by the warm wind of his creative tenderness.

Fourteenth Station
ENTOMBMENT

'Come down from the cross if you are the Son of God.'

He has. So have we. This is where the road goes. Our human effort has been spent and we do not have to walk any more.

Waiting is not a goal. Waiting is expectation, and expectation is what life is for. We can do a lot, we can walk a long distance but the ultimate purpose of life is not walking but waiting. The trouble is not waiting but the quarrels we pick with it.

In our times of being spent, we try to see the point, or change what cannot be changed or generally make a mess of what we are supposed to be doing, which is not doing but waiting. There are times for doing and times for waiting, and even the times of doing must have their share of expectation.

But even waiting is not the goal. Something else is, something we are waiting for, something we can only be given, something we know will come.

Fifteenth Station
RESURRECTION

We like it this way. The brook has become a sea and on the shore Jesus is making breakfast for his friends. We feel no estrangement from his holy and glorious wounds. We belong.

Our trouble is recognizing the same scene in bungled chances, scraped nerve ends, and the tantrum a child throws just as the company arrives. Time betrays us. We picture Resurrection morning as clear, flawless, and fragrant. Most of all we think of it as afterwards. Everything bad is over. We are nice and so is everybody else.

We are right in recognizing the sea as beautiful. Some day we shall have it. But what we have now is beautiful too: the difference lies in its hiddenness. At the end of a day dismembered by uncongenial surprises or empty as a rusted tin can, we hear no gulls calling over the water, and we are glad enough to see the sun go down.

Such an evening is inadequately known by what we feel about it. Our eyes are held so that we cannot see the transfiguration of our often tawdry circumstances, our dog-eared selves. But we can believe and be grateful.

Stay with us, Lord, upon the beach in the morning, now and forever, Amen.

Stations of the Cross

Gerard Mackrell

History and Value of this Devotion

Since the time of the first Christian emperor, Constantine, at the beginning the fourth century Christians were able to find an outlet for their deepest religious feelings, centring on redemption, by retreading the path their Saviour trod from Pilate's house to Calvary. A thousand years later the Franciscans were entrusted with the care of these sacred sites, and, aware that few could reach them, the friars set up in their churches in Europe 'Stations of the Cross' – pictorial representations of Jesus on his 'Via Dolorosa'. The number of these stations varied, but in 1731 Pope Clement XII fixed the number at fourteen. Five of these describe incidents found in early tradition; nine are from the Gospel itself.

The chief purpose of this devotion is to show a response which is the exact opposite of the mockery to which Jesus was subjected during his doleful journey. So we try to stimulate by word and picture feelings which we think should have been felt by bystanders of the actual event. The devotion is essentially an attempt to undo spiritually, not the death of Jesus, but the reactions of those agents in that drama. This we do in several ways. First, by identifying ourselves with those representative of our fallen humanity who, out of despair, hatred, shattered hopes, ridiculed the very process of their redeeming. Secondly, by exciting – but not forcing – some sensitivity and gratitude for the infinite mercy shown in the heroically meek (the opposite of 'weak') demeanour of Jesus in his execution. Thirdly, to become aware of the fiendish mental and physical suffering of Jesus by really believing on the pulses that he was a man as well as God. Without constructing a blow-by-blow pseudo-eye-witness account, we must avoid swinging to the other extreme of the antiseptic approach where blood is un-smelled and screams unheard. Finally, we must reel from our own problems and anguish to the steadying example before us. And – most difficult of all – try to believe (in the 'Lord, I believe; help my unbelief' way of a stricken father) that all of this affects me.

The Dream of the Rood

'Listen, I want to recount the most excellent of
visions, and what I dreamed in the middle of the
night, when other mortals lay abed.
It seemed to me that a wondrous tree spreading
aloft, spun about with light, a most magnificent timber ...
Magnificent, the cross of victory,
and I am stained with sins ...
Then that noble tree spoke these words:
'Years ago – I still recall it –
I was cut down at the forest edge ...
They set me on a hill.
Then I saw the Lord of mankind
hasten with much fortitude,
for he meant to climb me.,
I did not dare break
against the word of the Lord.
The young man, who was almighty God,
stripped himself,
strong and unflinching.
He climbed the despised gallows,
courageous under the scrutiny of man,
since he willed to redeem mankind ...
Christ was on the cross.'

From the mid-ninth century Anglo-Saxon poem, 'The Dream of the
Rood', translation in *Anglo-Saxon Poetry*. Printed with kind permission
of David Campbell.

First Station

JESUS IS CONDEMNED TO DEATH

The death, the 'handing over', you so often predicted, Lord, is here. The process has begun. Your disciples have fled; one betrayed you. But even had they remained faithful, you would have been alone. Death, above all, is lonely. Individual, alone.

No disciples. Not even Scribes and Pharisees, nor priests and elders. They have done their worst; but they were of your own people. Now you are up against Rome; a 'kingdom of this world'. The Son of Man, who will come on the clouds of heaven to judge all, stands before a buffoon and coward, and by him is sentenced to death. The one who raised Lazarus is to be slaughtered. All will be over and done with for the Passover. Then will all be neat and tidy again. And all will rest on the Sabbath.

Many black sabbaths have been mine. Many times have I killed and buried what is good because it tormented me. Only to find that it will not stay buried, that it torments me still. Many times have I judged. I, a posturing fool, have had the brazen arrogance to demolish in seconds a reputation that has taken years to build. May God forgive me. May you forgive me. May those I have so grievously injured find the grace to forgive me. Make me do what I can to restore the damage done. Make me forgive others who have hurt me.

Lord Jesus, let me try to learn that my reputation is not everything. Let me learn that most difficult, yet most comforting, lesson; to be 'meek and lowly of heart', so that I 'shall find rest for my soul'.

You are blasphemously accused of blasphemy, Lord, by those who knew no better. Whom you forgave.

Pilate has washed his hands of you. He too is frightened of you. So very often you frighten me with your love. This fear is almost blasphemous. Lord, may your suffering and death, which I have head of so often, now be listened to. This time, Lord, convince me. Of your love. Never leave me alone.

Second Station
JESUS RECEIVES HIS CROSS

At last, Lord! At last you see in concrete form the shadow of the Thing that loomed larger and larger over you. The Cross. Many times you predicted it to us your disciples.

You spoke of it in fear; in warning; in realism; in inflexible determination to embrace it as fiercely as it embraced you. You spoke of it with a kind of love and triumph: 'And I, when I shall be lifted up from the earth, shall draw all men to myself.'

Do you really think that?

To the Jews a stumbling block; to the rest of us folly. Not folly when we see that Cross in our lives, and deaths. Nothing foolish about it in cancer wards, street accidents, suicides. But certainly a stumbling block.And folly if we seek suffering.

You did not invent the Cross, Lord. You did not invent cancer, or nervous breakdowns, or bereavement. You wept over the dead Lazarus; you let your mother week over you.

Take me down from my Cross and I shall believe. Often have I thought that, said it, screamed it, whined it. And sighed it. Yet some relief in seeing that Cross. Here it comes at last. Long amputated from a parent tree in some sweet-smelling forest, it brings forth the greatest fruit of all – our redemption.

Now you begin to carry that Cross which will soon carry you. The Way of the Cross begins here. But the Cross was always with you – in many other shapes.

Wave a wand, Lord. Not over my Cross, to make it disappear. But over me, to make my terror disappear, or come under my control. And my anger, and hatred, and despair.

Take pity on us, Lord, as we drag our pieces of timber after you.

Third Station
JESUS FALLS THE FIRST TIME

You seem determined, Lord, to prove that you are only human. Down you fall. No miraculous physical strength. Human indeed. But not 'only human'. You not only fall; you get up. We can all fall; not all of us can rise again. The fall does not rest you. The Cross and the ground squeeze you; knock the breath out of you. But not your dignity. Soon you will have to helped to carry that Cross. You are teaching me so many lessons, this time without saying a word. 'If a man will be my disciple let him take up his cross daily and follow me.'

Even if we fall daily, or every hour, we can still take up the Cross again.

Lord, I am afraid of my first fall being my last. Many never rise from the first fall. If we stay on the ground we cannot fall again. Perhaps suffering will forget about us and pass us by. If we stay down we can get no lower. If we forget our ideas we need not try to live up to them. We can watch others fall and rise and fall again; and we can sneer at their futile efforts; call them hypocrites. For we are 'humble'; on the ground.

Make me realise, Lord, that humility is feet, not face, on the ground. That when I know my weakness I can ask for your strength.

Make me overcome the embarrassment of falling; the sense of failure.

With dust mixed with blood you rise again. And move on to the next fall.

Make me stagger towards Calvary; not walk away jauntily from it. Even if my Cross is self-inflicted, it hurts. Even more so. Make it redeeming for me, Lord. It is too bad to waste. Let me not waste this suffering.

Fourth Station

JESUS MEETS HIS BLESSED MOTHER

A harrowing meeting this, Lord. You cannot just leave the world completely detached. You have the same inextricable heart-strings as we have. With all the heartaches they bring with them. This mother who bore you loved you as flesh of her flesh, her pride and joy. And you loved her. And so the anguish is even more refined. We know all about that. That love exacts a terrible price. No love without sorrow. But without the pain of sorrow, no delight of love. You suffer because your mother suffers to see you suffer. There is no end to it.

For Mary the frightful emptiness of bereavement, after the numbing shock of death. And what a death! And what a dying! Oxen and asses when you were born; human oxen and asses at your death.

You knew why you were dying, Lord. Perhaps Mary came close to this knowledge. But that suffering did not know. The hammer and nails could not have cared less. Or the screaming senses wracked with pain.

A resurrection would follow. But to rise from the dead you must be dead. The sword spoken about by Simeon is turned in your mother's heart and soul. Nothing was spared her; that would have spoiled the sacrifice.

In the Temple only the best of the flocks were killed. The same on Calvary; only the best.

Many graces were given Mary because she had suffered much. But the glances between mother and son spoke everything. Total understanding. And total sympathy. The face you first saw on this earth is the one which your memory takes out of this life. There are two dyings here; both out of love. And you both love the unlovely faces about you. The reason for the dying. You both love me.

Fifth Station

SIMON OF CYRENE HELPS JESUS
TO CARRY HIS CROSS

What Simon does not realise is that it is he who is being helped.
That Cross belongs to Simon, not to Jesus. It belongs to me. In that
wood is all the filth of sin; all the agony of guilt. All the love-hate
of being estranged from a God who loves us.

Simon does not know this. Nor do we. We say it; we do not
really know what we are saying. Not really know. Not on our
pulses.

Even now we listen like an audience; we watch like spectators.
But we are deeply involved. Somewhere on that Cross are our
problems. Above all our sins. Not as solid as that, unfortunately;
but there.

Unfortunately! Do we really believe that? Would we willingly
exchange guilt for suffering? In our enlightened moods we probably would. Deep down we would. But sometimes too deep.

Simon of Cyrene. No one cares who you were, or what you were
doing, or why you were chosen. Like Herod and Pilate you would
have remained unknown if it had not been for one you all thought
unknown and a nonentity. But I am less known; less important. Who
has heard of me? Even now?

You, Lord, will never forget me. You remembered me before I
was a memory, before I was born. From all eternity you loved me;
to all eternity you will love me. And humour me by letting me
think that I help you to carry your Cross. Simon was ordinary.
How lovely, Lord, to bring him out of obscurity when bringing
him out of the crowd. For it was you who brought him. And what
memories he must have had after the first shock of anger or
disgust. What happy memories! Perhaps he knew that it really
was his Cross which you were helping him to carry. As you still do
for all of us.

And we all need to be needed. We are needed.

Sixth Station
VERONICA WIPES THE FACE OF JESUS

Another unknown emerges from the crowd, this time willingly. And bravely. Braving ridicule rather than punishment. But outstanding in the best sense. Veronica is not afraid to stand out from the mainly hostile crowd. But other women besides her and Mary are mourning Jesus. He will not leave this world without some fond memories.

On Veronica's cloth, Lord, you leave the imprint of your face. On her heart a deeper impression. Man, made to the image and likeness of God, now has God's image made to the image and likeness of man.

More help from mere mortals? More emptying of your self? No, not this time. Not you being emptied, but Veronica being filled – with love. Not you, Lord, stooping to conquer; but Veronica rising to greet you. But we only rise by your grace. All our memories of you are about suffering. We see you most of all, almost entirely, on a Cross which you make into a crucifix. Even when you are risen the wounds are still in hands and feet. War wounds proudly displayed. Human wounds humbly obtained.

Veronica is moved with pity. Nothing makes us more human than that. She may not have known that you were being executed because of your pity. She did not need to know. She only knew the little she could do; and that she did fully and lovingly. Lord, I can see you face on Veronica's towel, but not in your creatures. Not in myself. Pity will only involve me, and that is not good for my health. I cannot believe that I shall only find my true self by losing it; by having the imprint of others on my heart. Some memories are seared into me like fire-brands; but they are few and selective. And not all of them pleasant. Loving and unloving memories jostle within me.

One impulsive act, Lord, and I will find you. And find myself in you.

Seventh Station

JESUS FALLS THE SECOND TIME

A second bone-shaking fall, obviously worse that the first. More entertainment for the bloodthirsty; and the agony is dragged out. Once again an attempt to raise the physical strength to the unbending will. The spirit is willing; the flesh weak. More blood and dust. No transfiguration this time; no angels to minister to you, Lord. Why did the early Church allow this tradition of falls to become part of your way of the Cross? Is it part of the mockery, like the crown of thorns, the purple cloak, the reed sceptre? Is this a continuation of the death of a clown? We can easily forget the effect of the mockery. We see only your quiet dignity as no more than it should be. But the mockery must have hurt. For you were a king, you were the Messiah; you did come 'to save others'. 'Himself he cannot save,' mouthed the crowd. Yourself you would not save. And you were saving them even while they said it.

We know few details, Lord, of what happened between Pilate and Calvary. But we do know that you had to carry your own means of execution. Towards our Salvation.

We know that in Gethsemane blood was drawn without the help of nails, or scourging, or crowning with thorns. Thorns rattled inside your head before they were hammered onto your head. In all this maltreatment you were too humble to be humiliated. Too determined to give up. Too much in love to see all this as wasted.

Lord give me love. Give me a sense of purpose. With these I too can drag myself up again. Without them, why should I even try? Why not die where I fall, by giving up the struggle? That would give me peace, the peace of surrender. But you came to bring, not that kind of peace, but a sword which I must use, not on others, as Peter did, but on myself through self-discipline. No crocodile tears for you, Lord. Only courage and endurance. That is your lesson for me here.

Eighth Station
JESUS CONSOLES THE WOMEN OF JERUSALEM

As if suffering is not painful enough we often have to apologize for it. We are sometimes afraid to die for fear of hurting others! Our sickness, our death, can be a cause of grief and suffering to others; or a nuisance to them. We cannot crawl away like animals an simply fade out. Even dying is complicated precisely by those who love us and want to help us. They are worse than our executioners; they twist the sword in the wound. If only they did not exist! We become angry with them. Why will they not give us our freedom? But once we are dead that is no longer our worry. These Holy Women who weep for you, Lord, are told by you to weep for themselves and their children. But they are already weeping for themselves. All grief is for ourselves, since it hurts those we love. And our love is part of us.

You said you came to turn members of a household against each other. Did you mean that we must not allow our feelings for those we love to come between us and you? How free we should be if that were possible. How much greater the love if at the same it saved our freedom.

Yet in your agony you have time and love to console those who try to console you; because theirs is the greater need. Is there never to be any rest for you? Will crowds always pester you for healing, even now when you are half-dead yourself?

'Jesus had pity on the multitude because they were harrassed, like sheep without a shepherd. And he taught them many things.'

That was when you were tired and hungry, Lord. Now you are dying, and still you teach, console, encourage. Make me worth it. At least, make me less unworthy.

Ninth Station
JESUS FALLS THE THIRD TIME

The third and last fall. The next time to lie on the ground, Lord, you will be a corpse. The agony is now reaching a climax; yet it will soon be over. All these steps from Bethlehem to this. Never faltering. Teaching us to forgive, to love, to die in order to live. And now, more than ever, teaching us by example.

But what a price! Flattened again on the ground. Your tormentors nervous lest you die on them before the Cross you are carrying carries you. But you will not cheat the gallows.

'Greater love has no man, than that he lay down his life for his friends.'

'For the Son of Man came to serve, not to be served; and to give his life as a ransom for many.'

Lord, this third fall is your last. It seems so distant and meaningless to me. Leaves me quite unmoved; I have heard all this so often. But when it happens to me, when I think that this is my last fall, I panic or despair.

Not my last fall in the sense that I shall never fall again; but my last fall in the sense that I shall never get up again.

I sometimes feel that aches and pains herald my imminent death, and I cannot think of you, be encouraged by you. Then the fear passes and I do not want to think of you.

Lord, my life is so precarious. My friends die around me; my family is thinned out by the scythe of that 'grim reaper', whom you are soon to confront. May I see your third and last fall rather as your third and final rising from the dust. Not in your glory, but in your dust and sweat. You did not fall again after this. Your last act before Calvary was not falling, but rising from a fall. There is the glimmer of an Easter even here. I must rise many times in dust and sweat, if I am to rise with you in glory.

Tenth Station
JESUS IS STRIPPED OF HIS CLOTHES

Naked we came into the world, naked we leave it. But not like this. In the stable wrapped in swaddling clothes; here stripped of all clothes. Soon to be stripped of life itself. Your naked soul with soon slip from its house of the body. Now the final debasement; yet which is your willing abasement. You are not humiliated. Lord; you are beginning your exaltation.

Soon all pretence will be stripped from all of us. Soon the harsh glare of judgment will penetrate through the layers of disguise much thicker than clothing.

So often our pretences are burial clothes which smother us. And the cold air we shrink from is life-giving. But to our naked self, so sensitive to anything like the truth, the gentle air is abrasive.

Lord, I need some self-deception to get me through life. I need reassuring, affirmation; and I need to give these to others. But wean me from the need of the flattery and self-deception which stifle me. Which do me harm, make me really foolish. And not a harmless, but a destructive, folly. Lord, before the final detachment of death, give me a spirit of detachment from what does not last anyway; from what will leave me before I leave it. Give me that sense of values which glues me to what is lasting. Unfasten my grip on what is shifting and non-supporting.

Soon all will be switched off: sun, moon, sky, trees, loved ones; as I slide into eternity. Save me from the nakedness of loneliness.

Make me aware, Lord, of the homeless, of all without shelter, of the poorly-clad, the hungry. I must make a greater effort to shed luxuries to give others necessities. Peel from me, Lord, the pathetic rags and tatters of my attachments. Give me a healthy independence from escapist drugs, drink, over-eating, over-dressing; while thankfully using the developments modern science has made to relieve suffering and ease my passage through life. Not one bit of my body is not in the earth to which I shall return. May that both sober and console me.

Eleventh Station
JESUS IS NAILED TO THE CROSS

The indignity and shame of crucifixion mean little compared to the physical pain. No quick execution for you. No being dispatched. A dying as well as a death. Three hours to endure. Three long hours, long as years, to grasp that you are not executed but being executed. And Pilate thought that three hours was short. But Pilate never hung there.

But the mockery is still not completed. On this combination of pillory and gallows is the 'titulus' Proclaiming you 'King of the Jews'.

King of Kings, Lord of Lords, hammered and nailed to a Cross, we too know the meaning of agony. Unlike you, we cannot support it; unlike you, we also inflict it.

'And I, when I am lifted up from the earth, will draw all men to myself.'

We look at the crucifix, Lord, and we are not drawn. Not the cross you died on, but the cross on which we are spread-eagled. We do not see them as uplifting, but crushing us down. Make me realise, Lord, the value that suffering can have; I already know its destructive power. How it can degrade is known to all of us; how it can weaken or extinguish faith. Show us its purifying power. Give us a meaning and motive. Hammer this meaning into us like nails.till it draws blood. Then we shall not be mystified; only terrified. As you were frightened. Give us a meaning.

Lord, there are many bones stretched on crosses by me. Many bleed a little inside because of wounds I inflict, either through malice or stupid insensitivity. Make me aware of the vulnerability of others before it is too late. Pardon and prevent the mockery I heap on the already over-burdened. Impaled like an insect, Lord of heaven and earth, you die in fiendish agony that makes you scream. 'My God, my God, why have you deserted me?' Then, Lord, you were on my level. That I understand. That I have shouted after pin-pricks, not nails. We shall never explore your empty spaces of utter loneliness in that cry of desolation. But we feel too closely nailed to a cross, and too far detached from God. Let us see our cross as our closeness to you. There your soul was divorced from your body; there you married us.

Twelfth Station
JESUS DIES ON THE CROSS

Even after a lingering dying it is hard to take in death. Even for us mortals. That very name describes us by saying that we will die. It leap-frogs over our birth, life, achievements, failures, as if they never were. Mortals. 'The ones who will die.' We who are about to die salute you, Lord.

Jesus dies on the Cross. Not 'Died' but 'dies'. But there is no such thing as dying, Lord. Just 'died'. One second you are alive; another second, another fraction of a second, and you are not alive. Jesus died on the Cross.

No clawing back anyone from death. The Last Enemy. The Great Leveller, The Futiliser, who makes all human endeavour trivial. Lord of the living and dead, you could have avoided death. But that was not the Father's plan. You conquered death for us; not for yourself. You cut Death down to size, not by evading it, but by enduring it. By challenging Death to do its worst. And when it did so, there was no anaesthetic. you looked Death in the eye, until Death closed your eyes. Then, when Death had finished with you, Death itself died.

'He led captivity captive.' You killed Death, Lord. You desecrated graveyards and tombstones, crematoria, rottenness and corruption, where darkness yielded to day, where the Sabbath rest gave way to the noise and activity of work and waking. You trivialised Death. You, who were stripped of clothes, of body, stripped Death of its mystery; stripped us of our terror and superstition. 'Into your hands, Father, I commend my spirit.' So you sigh your soul to God. So you breathe your spirit upon us. Your death is our life. You who breathed your life into the Father's hands breathed into man a living soul.

Lord, a corpse is so empty, a mockery of what it once was. Utterly detached and enigmatic. The greatest challenge to our faith. It empties us, pours us out like water. Give us comfort and faith in the face of death, of bereavement; give us contempt for death, and love and hope for the dead. The mortals are also immortals. For you led captivity captive. And set captives free.

Thirteenth Station
JESUS IS TAKEN DOWN FROM THE CROSS

Lord, it really is consummated now. Your love is smeared with the blood over that Cross. That Cross is a poultice which has sucked out through your wounds the venom of the whole of sinful humanity. The Cross is thrown on the rubbish tip like a blood-splattered bandage; what is left of you has been disentangled from it. A lifeless heap.

'Truly this was the Son of God.'

More unexpected than an earthquake. Who shouted that?

The leader of the execution squad!

And when?

Not when you were walking on water, Not when you raised the dead to life. Not when you spoke so movingly about God and man, and life and death.

But now! After you had shouted in a loud voice, 'My God, my God, why have you deserted me.' Then came the cry of faith. Some people are like that. Suffering bravely borne, defeat gracefully accepted, impress them more than success. They have been 'there' themselves. You find the chink in their armour; you touch a responsive chord within them.

When you barely resembled a man, this centurion was hailing you as God. At least a very great man; to a Roman more than a god, as he would understand God. But you change your bait for each of us, Lord. You learned something from those fishermen of yours.

And still on his Cross is that 'Good Thief' you snatched from hell as the flames were licking his heels.

And now, Lord, where are you?

'He descended into hell.' The harrowing of hell. But you have just come from the hell of Calvary. You descended into a kind of hell when you became man; at Nazareth, at Bethlehem. And you made that hell a heaven on earth for those who believed in you.

Lifeless one, give me life. Real, vibrant life filled with love and purpose. Blast me out of this tomb of selfishness. Make me hack my way out of me to you and others.

Fourteenth Station
JESUS IS LAID IN THE TOMB

'And on the seventh day God rested.'

We are now completely out of our depth, Lord. Creeds cannot formulate what is happening to you now.What you are happening to others.

From womb to tomb. The cycle is completed. The warm darkness before life to the cold darkness after life.

'We were buried with him by baptism into death, so that as Christ was raised from the dead by the glory of the Father, we too might walk in newness of life.'

You remain in that tomb, Lord, on the seventh day. As soon as the sabbath is ended – and not a minute longer, that tomb is empty. 'But on the first day of the week, at early dawn, they went to the tomb, taking the spices... And they found the stone rolled away from the tomb but when they went in they did not find the body.' And they felt even emptier at the empty tomb.

But the body found them. In your Risen Glory, Lord, you showed the wounds made by the nails. They too were glorious. Your suffering was glorious; your tomb a palace. your tomb the womb of your glory. That tomb's emptiness is our fullness.

Lord, when I am numbed by failure, or petrified in boredom, or paralysed by fear, make me see the gleam of glory. Give me hope when it is most needed.

Make me roll away that stone behind which I quietly wither. My own tomb beckons. It too is no more an abiding city than the present. Death is shorter than life.

Lord, give me strength in the steps to my death, in my walk to Calvary. In those stops I may make; the blood-tests, X-rays, fearful nights in hospital, the pain on the faces of loved ones, the anger that I am too young or unprepared. And when others are taken from me, let me see the terrible empty places as the emptiness of your tomb.

'If Christ be not risen, then is our faith in vain.' But you are risen, Lord. So everything has meaning and hope. I ask for help, in the name of the Father who made me, in the name of the Son who redeemed me, in the name of the Holy Spirit who sanctified me. Amen.

A Missionary
Way of the Cross

Seán P. Kealy

Introduction

When we were young we were probably amazed at the wicked-
ness of everybody involved in Jesus' crucifixion – Pilate, Caiaphas
and the priests, the crowds, the cowardly disciples, Judas who
betrayed him.

We would have been quite different. The experience of life, as
we try to continue the mission of Jesus, has probably altered our
attitude. Now we realize that those who crucified Jesus were
people like ourselves, people full of selfishness, problems and
fears. I could be any of those all too human people facing uncertain
choices and acting out of unpredictable passions. The old question
'Were you there when they crucified my Lord' now elicits a
different, more humble response: 'Yes, Lord, It is I'.

Mission is the following of Christ as he takes away the sins of the
whole world including my own. To follow is to deny one's self and
ambitions, to take up a similar cross and to follow Christ's way of
life, his values, his attitude to the Father, his love reaching out even
unto enemies.

Let us pray:

O Jesus, my Brother, how often I have made these Stations yet
how seldom I recognise your Stations once I leave the church. Help
me to stop crucifying you in my life and to recognise you especially in the poor and the afflicted wherever they are in our world.

First Station

JESUS CONDEMNED TO DEATH

Is 50:5f; Mt 27:11-13; Phil 2:5-11

Judge not, said Jesus. But he is being unjustly judged so often in so many countries of our world for his colour, his creed, his poverty, by people like myself. We have no reason to feel superior to Judas who betrayed Jesus because we are all guilty of betraying him in our relationships and activities.

Let us pray:

Jesus our Brother, what a dreadful mistake, we say so easily, when we see you condemned to death, that Pilate and the Jewish leaders and crowds did not recognise that you were the Son of God. Everybody is called to be a son of God. Help us to see you in our neighbour whether innocent or guilty and to stop committing the same injustices in our world of today.

Second Station

JESUS TAKES UP HIS CROSS

Is 53:6-8; 1 Cor 1:18-25; Mt 27:27-31; Mk 8:34-35

Look at the innocent Jesus taking up with his Cross the sufferings of the world. Suffering is an essential part of the lives of all men and women everywhere. Jesus gives the example and the courage to us to take up the cross of caring for a handicapped child, of living confined to a bed or a wheelchair, of old age and its loneliness and dependence. The world is full of suffering, innocent and guilty. Jesus makes a difference to the suffering of the world by joining all in their grief and pain.

Let us pray:

O God our Father, Jesus invited us to take up our Cross and to follow. We pray for courage to unite our suffering with the sufferings of all people without exception as we pray for all the peoples of the world that they may become one with your suffering Son in their journey to you.

Third Station
JESUS FALLS THE FIRST TIME

Jn 12:23-24; Heb 2:17-18; 1 Cor 1:23-25

Jesus empties himself so much that he can go no further. In John's Gospel Jesus warns us that to love life is to lose it but to hate one's life in this world is to keep it for eternal life. For if a person serves him he must follow him: where he is his servants will be there also. But Jesus keeps going. What is difficult is not to begin but to summon up the courage to continue when all seems hopeless.

Let us pray:
O Jesus, it is so easy to see you in the strong, the enthusiastic, the good. Help us to see you struggling in the poor, the sick, the weak, the sinners whatever their nationality or creed. Give us your patient endurance as you reached out to the divorced Samaritan, Mary Magdalen, as you called Judas Friend.

Fourth Station
JESUS MEETS HIS MOTHER

Lk 1:46-55; Lam 2:13; Jn 16:20-22

In the Gospels Mary is the first Christian disciple not simply because of physical relationship to Jesus but because she met the gospel criterion that a disciple is one who does the will of God. But a disciple is also one who mourns the injustice of our world. Jesus carrying his cross meets many mothers as they live in the slums of our world, their sons and daughters without basic human rights, jobs or social help, compelled to eke out their depressing existence in appalling conditions.

Let us pray:

Jesus, our Brother, help us to realise that the world is our home, that all peoples are our brothers. Help us to reach out beyond our own natural family, our narrow circle of friends, to the many suffering Marys of our world and their children who are our brothers and sisters, our sons and daughters.

Fifth Station

SIMON OF CYRENE HELPS JESUS CARRY HIS CROSS

Lk 23:26; Mt 11:28-30; 1 Pet 4:13-16

Surprisingly, after all whom Jesus himself had helped, a man had to be forced to help him carry his cross – Simon from Africa. Palestine was an occupied country and a Roman officer had only to touch a person on the shoulder to compel him to help. Help Jesus carry his cross in our world is the request to each of us. Who me? I do not want to get involved. I have so much to do for my family, job, friends, club, Church. So often we only grudgingly get involved but Jesus speaks to us: My yoke is sweet.

Let us pray:

Father, help us to see the sufferings of Jesus in our world and so become willingly involved. Help us to show that we deserve the name of Christian. We pray that wherever there are people suffering from hatreds, conflicts or any kind of injustice Christians will not be afraid to suffer for peace and reconciliation.

Sixth Station

VERONICA WIPES THE FACE OF JESUS

Mt 25:35-40; Is 53:2-5; Gal 6:2

A woman has the courage to become involved with Jesus. Veronica, whose Greek name means victory-bringer, is not mentioned in the gospels. At dinner in the house of a Pharisee Jesus does not even receive the normal courtesies (Lk 7:36-50). But a sinful woman shows her love by anointing Jesus with her most precious possession. The suffering of Jesus should provoke us to respond with deeds of love. The suffering face of Jesus is imprinted on so many people and situations in our world.

Let us pray:

Father, we pray for all who suffer in our world. We pray too for all who care for the sick, for prisoners for the lonely, the dying May all, especially Christians, open their hearts with generosity and without counting the cost, to give themselves to create a world of friendship, respect and brotherly love.

Seventh Station

JESUS FALLS THE SECOND TIME

Lk 23:44; Ps 43:25-27; 108:25-27

It is difficult to identify with a fallen Jesus. Naturally I prefer the strong kind Jesus but the weak exhausted Son of God is a problem for me. So many of his followers in our world are exhausted. Think of the coffee and tea we enjoy so much. Yet is is picked generally by poor women toiling all day in the hot sun for mere subsistence wages.

Let us pray:

Lord, we believe that the cries of the workers whose wages have been kept back unjustly, have reached your ears. We too confess that we have made you suffer by our many injustices. Help us to remember that to persecute your people is to persecute you. Teach us to be more aware of the injustices which we cause in our world.

Eighth Station

JESUS COMFORTS THE WOMEN OF JERUSALEM

Lk 23:27-28; Mt 13:55; Jn 4:10-24

Jesus' compassionate words are a Jewish way of saying: 'Weep not so much for me as for yourselves and for your children.' Jesus was no magician who claimed to banish all human sufferings and problems with the wave of a magic wand. Often it is the women and children who suffer the most. Jesus invites the women to be concerned with their own sufferings, to take up their own cross. Even in the midst of his own sufferings he reaches out to others with his paradox: Blessed are those who mourn.

Let us pray:

Jesus our Brother, help us to comfort, to give strength to those in need, to reach out to you as you suffer once again in our world especially in the women and in the helpless children of our world. Some seventeen million children die of malnutrition in our world each year and we are so comfortable and so concerned with our minor problems.

Ninth Station

JESUS FALLS THE THIRD TIME

Jn 15:9-17; Ps 37:7-11; 1 Pet 2:22-24

We are reduced to silence once more at the thought of Jesus overwhelmed by the cross of his great love for all people. Love one another as I have loved you is his command if one can call it a command. It is more like the helpless plea of the one who first loved us, who gave his every moment to wash away our sins and unhappiness. According to St Paul, in his weakness he learned to appreciate the words of Jesus: 'My grace is enough for you: my power is at its best in weakness' (2 Cor 12:9).

Let us pray:

Jesus, while no one could accuse you of sin, yet you learned to sympathise with our weakness. Although you were God's Son you learned to obey and to become perfect through suffering. Help us to learn from our own sufferings to reach out to the sufferings of others and thus to become more like you.

Tenth Station

JESUS IS STRIPPED OF HIS CLOTHING

Jn 19:23-24; Ps 22:16-19; Is 61:10

They divided his clothing into four shares but cast lots for his seamless garment: 'Instead of tearing it, let us throw dice to decide who is to have it'. The High Priest wore a seamless garment woven in one piece when he offered sacrifice for the people. Jesus' garment symbolised the unity which he died to bring to all peoples.

Let us pray:

O God, as we consider Jesus stripped and bare, help us to realise that his stripping is still going on in our world, in his and our brothers, in the starving children of the African deserts, the untouchables of India, the oppressed minorities everywhere – the list is endless. Teach us to share not just our abundance but to be willing even to be stripped of our necessities.

Eleventh Station

JESUS IS NAILED TO THE CROSS

Jn 19:17-22; Lk 23:33-34; Gal 5:22-24

In Guatemala Pope John Paul II told the people:

> When you trample a man, when you violate his rights, when you commit flagrant injustices against him, when you submit him to torture, break in and kidnap him or violate his right to life you commit a crime and a grave offence against God.

Jesus is continually being nailed in our world as people are locked away in jails for their beliefs and forgotten by the rest of the comfortable; as he is locked in mental hospitals and old peoples' homes, where there is a shortage of money for adequate care. Yet God made a wonderful world, a veritable Garden of Eden with plenty for all to share and this is how we respond by crucifying him again.

Let us pray:

> Jesus our Brother, forgive us for nailing you down so often with our selfishness. Help us to use your wonderful world and all our talents for the good of all, particularly the poor, the handicapped, even those whose beliefs differ from our own.

Twelfth Station

JESUS DIES ON THE CROSS

Mt 27:50; Mk 15:37; Lk 23:46; Jn 19:28-30

Death is a great fact in all of our lives, our greatest fear. In his Saint John Passion, J. S. Bach invites us:

> Haste to Golgotha, O take the wings of faith and fly to the Cross of Jesus, to find relief and healing there.

The nearer we come to the Cross of Jesus the nearer people come to one another. Jesus' Cross is the place where we can be brought together and made more deeply one than in any other place. Each gospel has a different interpretation of the tremendous significance of his 'crucial' event. Luke's narrative is proposed as an example for us to follow in our own deaths.

'Father into your hands I commend my Spirit.'

Many Christian martyrs such as Stephen and the English martyrs used this phrase before their execution.

Let us pray:

Jesus, you taught us that unless the grain of wheat dies, it remains alone. Help us to have the courage to commit our lives to the Father so that others may enjoy a more abundant life.

Thirteenth Station

JESUS IS TAKEN DOWN FROM THE CROSS

Jn 19:38; Rom 8:10-11; Is 12:1-3

Like so many mothers in our world, Mary receives the dead body of her son taken down from the Cross. Who can describe their thoughts as they are helped by well meaning strangers such as Joseph of Arimathaea, the secret disciple or Nicodemus who came by night. The death of Jesus gives these men the courage to come out into the open. What sorrow can be compared to the sorrow of this occasion. Yet similar brutal and useless killings have been piercing mothers' hearts ever since.

Let us pray:

Father, help the leaders of our world to learn that killing is not any answer to the problems of our world. Help people of violence to change, to trust in the power of love not guns, to accept the way of loving service and forgiveness. O Death where is your victory? O Death, where is your sting?

Fourteenth Station

JESUS IS LAID IN THE TOMB

Jn 19:38-42; Mt 27:57-61; Rom 6:8-23

We so easily bury Jesus in our thoughts, words and deeds. We live with him in our prayers, in Church, but as he lives in our brothers and sisters we so often bury him. Yet even in death he is at work, tearing apart the veil of separation between God and people, between people of different kinds, raising the dead. Jesus wants to continue working in our lives. As Teresa of Avila said to her community: 'Christ has no body now on earth but yours, no hands but yours, no feet but yours. Yours are the eyes through which Christ's compassion looks out on humankind. Yours are the feet with which he is to walk the ways of the world. Yours are the hands with which he is to bless us now.'

Let us pray:

Jesus, come and live in and through us. Help us to realise that all we do affects your reaching out to our neighbour. Help us to love with your love.

Fifteenth Station

EPILOGUE

There is a happy ending. The Christ we have followed did not remain in the tomb. He rose. He is alive and so can we be. The old Via Dolorosa in Jerusalem leads to the Church of the Holy Sepulchre which our Greek brothers prefer to name the Church of the Resurrection. All the gospels culminate in the resurrection and each account leads to the missionary command of the risen Jesus to his disciples. If we have really followed Jesus and meditated on what he has done for us, we will want to share the joyful news that we have found a compassionate Saviour and Redeemer.

Fifteenth Station

Let us pray:

Father, help us to really believe that the Jesus who suffered and died for all people is alive. As we have followed him in his sufferings help us to follow him and to lead others to the glory of his Resurrection. Help us to be Easter people who face the sufferings of life with hope and joy knowing that Jesus our brother is alive.

A West Indian
Way of the Cross

June Johnston & Glenroy Taitt

Foreword

The Way of the Cross is not only about the journey to Calvary that
Jesus made two thousand years ago. It is also our journey. As we
meditate on the Way of the Cross we reflect on life – our personal
lives, the lives of others, our country and the whole world.

Appropriate hymns should be sung at the beginning and end of
the service and at suitable points between stations. The prayers
given are meant only as starters. Leaders may invite the people to
add their own silent prayer or to pray out loud.

First Station

JESUS IS CONDEMNED TO DEATH

'Her is your King!' said Pilate to the Jews. 'Take him away, take him away!' they said. 'Crucify him!' (Jn 19:15).

Meditation
Today we condemn Jesus to death in: the physically handicapped, the blind, the hearing impaired, the mentally retarded, the elderly. We fail to make them full members of our our communities.

Prayer
Lord, you call us to protect these least of our brothers and sisters. Forgive us for the times when we have been like the crowd shouting 'crucify him, crucify him'.

Second Station

JESUS TAKES UP HIS CROSS

They then took charge of Jesus, and carrying his own cross he went out of the city to the skull, or as it is called in Hebrew, Gologtha. (John 19:17)

Meditation
Let us think of all those who bear crosses: women who have been raped and must live with that memory; parents with retarded children; a family in which the bread-winner has been retrenched and is unable to find another job; children with alcoholic parents.

Prayer
We pray for all those who bear crosses. May they experience Jesus walking with them as they struggle with their cross.

Third Station

JESUS FALLS THE FIRST TIME

For though the virtuous man falls seven time, he stands up again,
the wicked are the ones who stumble in adversity. (Prov 24:16).

Meditation

Let us think of people who experience their first fall: husbands or
wives who have been unfaithful to their partners; public figures
who preach high ideals and yet are weak in some area of their
private lives; someone who enters politics or trade unionism and
then finds himself making compromises.

Prayer

We pray for all those who have experienced their first fall. May the
first fall of Jesus remind them that they need not give up their high
ideals. May they accept the challenge to stand again.

Fourth Station

JESUS MEETS HIS AFFLICTED MOTHER

Near the cross of Jesus stood his mother and his mother's sister,
Mary the wife of Clopas, and Mary of Magdala. John 19:25

Meditation

Mary lives int eh afflicted mothers who watch their children carry
a cross: mothers who see their children go to prison or even
condemned to death; mothers who watch their children die form
illness; mothers who watch while their children are misunderstood, unfairly criticized and humiliated; mothers whose children
are drug addicts, homosexuals, or lesbians.

Prayer

Lord, we thank you for the Marys of today, the courageous women
whom you call to stand by the cross on which their children are
being crucified.

Fifth Station

SIMON OF CYRENE HELPS JESUS TO CARRY HIS CROSS

As they were leading him away they seized on a man, Simon from Cyrene, who was coming in from the country, and made him shoulder the cross and carry it behind Jesus. Luke 23:26

Meditation
Let us think of those who are Simon of Cyrene today: teachers who give extra attention to slow learners; the worker who is Simon of Cyrene for his or her fellow-workers; groups who are Simon of Cyrene to the young people who have been considered failures; organizations which provide for the homeless; countries which assist other countries in times of natural disasters.

Prayer
We thank you, Lord, for calling on men and women to shoulder the cross and carry it behind Jesus. We thank you that they answer this call with courage and dignity.

Sixth Station

VERONICA WIPES THE FACE OF JESUS

'But you', he said, 'who do you say I am?' Luke 9:20

Meditation
We would like to live at peace with all, we want a good life without conflict. Veronica preserves on her towel the disfigured face of Jesus. She is the preacher who shows up our compromises, the hungry children, the disfigured bodies we see on the tv., the people we have hurt because we took the easy way out. Hide from it as we try, Veronica still shows the world the face of Jesus.

Prayer

We pray for all those who must be Veronicas in the world today.
Give them courage to preserve the towel and be always ready to
show the true face of Jesus to those who seek him.

Seventh Station

JESUS FALLS THE SECOND TIME

It was essential that he should in this way become completely like
his brothers so that he could be a compassionate and trustworthy
high priest of God's religion, able to atone for human sins. He-
brews 2:17

Meditation

In this fall Jesus experiences the weakness of his brothers and
sisters: we see in him people of power who freely choose to walk
with little people, sharing their frustrations; the adults who confess their mistakes and failures to the young, and ask for their
forgiveness and encouragement; in Church leaders who search for
the truth along with everyone else, experiencing pain and the
anxieties that are common to all; teachers who toil side by side
with their students, helping and being helped by them.

Prayer

We thank you, Lord, for those leaders who keep alive in the world
today Jesus' way of authority. We pray especially for the Church
that in our communities Jesus may be the model for all leaders.

Eighth Station

JESUS SPEAKS TO THE WOMEN OF JERUSALEM

Large numbers of people followed him, and of women too, who mourned and lamented for him. But Jesus turned to them and said: 'Daughters of Jerusalem, do not weep for me; weep rather for yourselves and for your children'. Luke 23:27-28

Meditation

Let us think of those today who turn to us with the message 'weep not for me; weep rather for yourselves and for your children': the persons afflicted with a terminal illness whose spirit is not crushed but who teaches us, the strong and the healthy, how to treasure the gift of life; a blind person who shows us that we are closing our eyes to the truth; the family that chooses to live a simple life-style and must face the scepticism of friends and relatives, but their way of life challenges our consumer society.

Prayer

We thank you, Lord, for those people who, when we would console them, turn and challenge us to examine our lives.

Ninth Station

JESUS FALLS THE THIRD TIME

'I have toiled in vain, I have exhausted myself for nothing' Isaiah 49:4

Meditation

Jesus is falling today in those who are being crushed by others: people who live under dictatorships; battered wives; children habitually abused by their parents or guardians;people so insulted and rejected that they have neither self-confidence nor self-respect.

Prayer

Lord, we pray for all those who remain in despair by the weight of their cross. We pray that, like Jesus, they may get up again knowing their cause is with the Lord and their reward with God.

Tenth Station

JESUS IS STRIPPED OF HIS GARMENTS

When they had finished crucifying him they shared out his clothing by casting lots. Matthew 27:35

Meditation

Today Jesus is stripped of his garments whenever people are stripped of their dignity: children made to feel failures by parents because they fail their examination; elderly people when they are treated harshly at government offices; people whose culture was looked down upon by the Church and the colonising countries.

Prayer

Forgive us for the time when we too strip others of their dignity. You call us to clothe the naked. Help us to be people who encourage others to grow in awareness of their dignity as children of God.

Eleventh Station

JESUS IS NAILED TO THE CROSS

The people stayed there watching him. As for the leaders, they jeered at him. 'He saved others', they said, 'let him save himself if he is the Christ of God, the Chosen One'. Luke 23:35-36

Meditation

Let us think of those who have been nailed to a cross: the worker who tries to organize his colleagues and is therefore victimized; the female employee who refuses to give in to the advances of her boss and suffers victimization or loses her job; those imprisoned for their commitment to a free South Africa.

Prayer

Lord, we thank your for those people whom you have called to be nailed to the cross. Forgive us for the times when we too have been among the leaders jeering at them.

Twelfth Station

JESUS DIES ON THE CROSS

'Father, into your hands I commit my spirit'. With these words he breathed his last. Luke 23:46

Meditation

Let us think of those who, like Jesus, have died on a cross: martyrs like Mahatma Gandhi, Martin Luther King, Archbishop Romero, Maximilian Kolbe; our ancestors who died struggling against their oppressors, the silent prophet, the artist, the craftsman/ woman whose talents have died under the cross of cultural domination.

Prayer

Lord, we thank you for the witness of these people. We thank you that they, having lived and died like Jesus, have become a source of life for us.

Thirteenth and Fourteenth Stations

JESUS IS TAKEN DOWN FROM THE CROSS AND PLACED IN THE TOMB

Having been assured of this by the centurion, he granted the corpse to Joseph who bought a shroud, took Jesus down from the cross, wrapped him in the shroud and laid him in a tomb which had been hewn out of the rock. Mark 15:45-46

Meditation

Let us think of those today who have been taken down from their own cross and placed in a tomb: parents in their old age abandoned by their children, and who now see the sacrifices they made as futile; workers suddenly made redundant after working for a company for over twenty years; people in places like Northern Ireland and the Middle East who live daily with war and who see no immediate prospect of peace.

Prayer

Lord, teach us what it is to endure in faith the emptiness of the tomb. Save us from despair. Help us to realise that it is in silence and darkness, in the womb and in the earth, that new life forms.

Fifteenth Station

JESUS RISES FROM THE DEAD

Terrified, the women lowered their eyes. But the two men said to them, 'Why look among the dead for someone who is alive? he is not here, he has risen.' Luke 24:5-6

Meditation

Today Jesus rises from the dead in: former drug addicts who no assist in rehabilitation programmes; a backward student who, through the attention of a concerned and dedicated teacher, discovers that he or she can learn; people who can live creatively

---

with their cross whatever it may be.

Prayer
We thank you, Lord, for the resurrection moments of our lives –
the times of hope and joy when we can truly exclaim, 'He is no here,
he has risen!'

A Way of the Cross
for Religious

Conor O'Riordan

Introdcution

We will make the stations in the light of the Gospel of St Matthew.

Reading   Matthew 25.31-46

Pause for reflection

Now let us listen to how Pope John Paul II would apply this passage to contemporary life.

> By his Incarnation [Christ] the Son of God, in a certain way united himself with each man'. (*Gaudium et Spes*, 22) ... We are not dealing with the 'abstract' man, but the real, 'concrete', 'historical' man. We are dealing with 'each' man, for each one is included in the mystery of the Redemption and with each one Christ has united himself for ever through this mystery. Every man without any exception whatever has been redeemed by Christ, with man – with each man without any exception whatever – Christ is in a way united even when man is unaware of it. 'Christ, who died and was raised up for all, provides man' – each man and every man – 'with the light and the strength to measure up to his supreme calling ... ' (Gaudium et Spes, 10). This responsibility becomes especially evident for us Christians when we recall and we should always recall it – the scene of the last judgement according to the words of Christ related in St Matthew's Gospel. This eschatological scene must always be 'applied' to man's history; it must always be made the 'measure' for human acts as an essential outline for an examination of conscience by each and every one.
>
> *Redemptor Hominis*, 13

First Station

JESUS IS JUDGED AND CONDEMNED

Do we not imitate Pilate when we condemn Christ unjustly in his members? What about our hasty judgement of superiors, our readiness to judge harshly our fellow religious without knowing all the facts?

Remember, that Jesus said: 'Truly I say to you, as you did it to one of the least of these, my brethren, you did it to me'.

V. Jesus our Brother, forgive us.

R. For we know not what we do.

Second Station

JESUS ACCEPTS THE CROSS

We admire the generosity and self-sacrifice of Jesus as he accepts the cross. Can we not spare a word of encouragement for him now as in his members he accepts the crosses of old age, illness, insecurity or indeed the cross of service in our congregation.?

Remember, Jesus said: 'Truly I say to you, as you did it not to one of the least of these, you did it not to me'.

V. Jesus, our Brother, forgive us.

R. For we know not what we do.

Third Station

JESUS FALLS THE FIRST TIME

Our hearts melt with pity as we consider how Jesus fell beneath the burden of the cross. Yet are we not harsh towards him in his members? They sometimes fall under pressure of the crosses which they are asked to bear. We pity Jesus as he fell two thousand years ago. We too often despise him as he falls today.

Remember, Jesus said: 'Truly I say to you, as you did it to one of the least of these, my brethren you did it to me'.

V. Jesus, our Brother, forgive us.
R. For we know not what we do.

Fourth Station

JESUS MEETS HIS MOTHER

We pity the mother, we pity the Son. Are we sufficiently sensitive to the needs of those in sorrow? A caring presence can bring comfort and healing. Do we try to bring comfort to Christ in his sorrowing brothers and sisters by taking the time and trouble to be available to them?

Remember, Jesus said: 'Truly I say to you, as you did it not to one of the least of these, you did it not to me.'

V. Jesus, our Brother, forgive us.
R. For we know not what we do.

Fifth Station

SIMON IS FORCED TO HELP CARRY THE CROSS

We envy Simon the opportunity that was offered him, we may even criticise him for his reluctance to grasp the opportunity. Yet how often have we shied away from helping Christ in his members? Maybe it would be inconvenient, maybe it would involve us with weird characters. After all we must consider the good name of our institute, our own reputation. Are we too selective in offering help? We see Christ in some of his members but not in each man and woman without any exception whatever.

Remember, Jesus said: 'Truly I say to you, as you did it not to one of the least of these, you did it not to me'.

V. Jesus, our Brother, forgive us.
R. For we know not what we do.

Sixth Station

VERONICA WIPES THE FACE OF JESUS

Veronica braved the hostile crowd to give what help she could. Sometimes we lack the moral courage to come to the aid of Christ as he appears in an unpopular member of our community, an unattractive child in our school, a demanding patient in our hospital, a troublesome parishioner. We too easily forget how even a small expression of loving concern can make a hard life a little less dehumanising

Remember, Jesus said: 'Truly I say to you, as you did it not to one of the least of these, you did it not to me'.

V. Jesus our Brother, forgive us.

R. For we know not what we do.

Seventh Station

JESUS FALLS THE SECOND TIME

Jesus was willing to carry the cross but it was too much for him – he fell a second time. Do we try to see Jesus in those who fall often. Do we give them sufficient credit for the efforts which they make in between falls?•Do we help them to rise? On the road to Calvary the reason for the fall was obvious. When Jesus falls now in his members the reasons may be less obvious but he is there – in need of our sympathy and understanding.

Remember Jesus said: 'Truly I say to you, as you did it to one of the least of these, my brethren, you did it to me'.

V. Jesus our Brother, forgive us.

R. For we know not what we do.

Eighth Station

JESUS SPEAKS TO THE WOMEN OF JERUSALEM

Even in the midst of his own troubles Jesus could still be about his Father's business. Sometimes we become so immersed in self-pity that we forget God and neighbour. We neglect our responsibilities. We ignore the greater needs of our brothers and sisters who may be dependant on us for support.

Remember, Jesus said: 'Truly I say to you, as you did it not to one of the least of these, you did it not to me'.

V. Jesus our Brother, forgive us.

R. For we know not what we do.

Ninth Station

JESUS FALLS THE THIRD TIME

Jesus fell yet a third time. Again we are moved with pity. But today if in his members we find him falling too often we are quick to dub him a hopeless case. We regard him as a failure undeserving of our continued support. Jesus got up again and achieved great things. Through our compassionate attitude towards him in our brother and sisters he can still achieve great things in spite of human weaknesses, difficulties and obstacles of every kind.

Remember, Jesus said: 'Truly I say to you, as you did it to one of the least of these, my brethren, you did it to me'.

V. Jesus our Brother, forgive us.

R. For we know not what we do.

Tenth Station

JESUS IS STRIPPED OF HIS GARMENTS

We cringe at the thought of this humiliation yet how often have we subjected Jesus to it as we stripped the poor of their human dignity, as we stripped a pupil of his/her few shreds of self-esteem, as we humiliated a novice or a fellow religious before the community!

Remember, Jesus said: 'Truly I say to you, as you did it to one of the least of these, my brethren, you did it to me'.

V. Jesus, our Brother, forgive us.

R. For we know not what we do.

Eleventh Station

JESUS IS NAILED TO THE CROSS

What barbarous treatment!. We mete it out to Christ when we keep him firmly nailed to the walls of our churches. When we refuse to see him in the slum dweller, the prisoner, the former priest, the ex-religious. We keep Jesus firmly nailed to the cross when we impede anyone in their growth towards their full human potential, when we make it difficult for them to measure up to their supreme calling.

Remember, Jesus said: 'Truly I say to you, as you did it to one of the least of these, my brethren you did it to me'.

V. Jesus, our Brother, forgive us.

R. For we know not what we do.

Twelfth Station

JESUS DIES ON THE CROSS

Jesus by dying you destroyed our death. Do we believe that? Do we make OUR faith in the life-giving death of Jesus a source of comfort to the dying? Once again Jesus cries out in them 'My God, my God, why hast thou forsaken me'? How do we respond? Are we too busy to bother? Are we so devoid of faith that we have nothing to offer?

Remember, Jesus Said: 'Truly I say to you, as you did it to one of the least of these, my brethren, you did it to me'.

V. Jesus, our Brother, forgive us.

R. For we know not what we do.

Thirteenth Station
JESUS IS TAKEN DOWN FROM THE CROSS

We may have become callous in the face of death – the death of others. When we conduct funerals or prayers for the dead, do we encourage hope? Do we strengthen faith in the paschal mystery and the resurrection of the dead? Are we sensitive to the mourners?

Remember, Jesus said: 'Truly I say to you, as you did it not to one of the least of these, you did it not to me'.

V. Jesus, our Brother, forgive us.

R. For we know not what we do.

Fourteenth Station
JESUS IS LAID IN THE TOMB

We keep Jesus buried in those who are entombed in mental hospitals, abandoned in old folks homes. Do we see him in those religious who by reason of an unsuitable assignment cannot use their many talents in the service of God and their neighbour? How often have we blighted the high ideals of the young in our schools, parishes or institutes through our cynicism and sarcasm?

Remember, Jesus said: 'Truly I say to you, as you did it to one of the least of these, my brethren, you did it to me'.

V. Jesus, our Brother, forgive us.

R. For we know not what we do.